TRUTH, TRIUMPH, and TRANSFORMATION*

*Formerly titled *The Truth about Attraction*

Also by Sandra Anne Taylor

Books

28 Days to a More Magnetic Life*

Secrets of Success: *The Science and Spirit of Real Prosperity,* with Sharon A. Klingler*

Quantum Success: *The Astounding Science of Wealth and Happiness**

Secrets of Attraction: *The Universal Laws of Love, Sex, and Romance**

Guided Visualizations, CDs, and Audio Programs

Act to Attract (nine-CD audio seminar and workbook)

Healing Journeys, including: *Cellular Regression: Timeless Healing* and *Relaxation and Memory Release* (CD)

Attracting Success, including: *Attracting Success* and *Planting Your Destiny Garden* (CD)

Act to Attract Meditations, including: *Attracting Love, Your Sacred Identity,* and *Morning and Evening Affirmations* (CD)

*Available from Hay House

Please visit:

Hay House USA: **www.hayhouse.com®**
Hay House Australia: **www.hayhouse.com.au**
Hay House UK: **www.hayhouse.co.uk**
Hay House South Africa: **www.hayhouse.co.za**
Hay House India: **www.hayhouse.co.in**

TRUTH, TRIUMPH, and TRANSFORMATION

Sorting Out the Fact from the Fiction in Universal Law

SANDRA ANNE TAYLOR

HAY HOUSE, INC.
Carlsbad, California • New York City
London • Sydney • Johannesburg
Vancouver • Hong Kong • New Delhi

Published and distributed in the United States by: Hay House, Inc.: www.hayhouse.com • ***Published and distributed in Australia by:*** Hay House Australia Pty. Ltd.: www.hayhouse.com.au • ***Published and distributed in the United Kingdom by:*** Hay House UK, Ltd.: www.hayhouse.co.uk • ***Published and distributed in the Republic of South Africa by:*** Hay House SA (Pty), Ltd.: www.hayhouse.co.za • ***Distributed in Canada by:*** Raincoast: www.raincoast.com • ***Published in India by:*** Hay House Publishers India: www.hayhouse.co.in

Editorial supervision: Jill Kramer • *Project editor:* Jessica Kelley
Design: Tricia Breidenthal

Library of Congress Cataloging-in-Publication Data

Taylor, Sandra Anne.
Truth, triumph, and transformation : sorting out the fact from the fiction in universal law / Sandra Anne Taylor. -- 1st ed.
p. cm.
ISBN 978-1-4019-1854-5 (pbk. : alk. paper) 1. Man-woman relationships. 2. Sexual attraction. 3. Interpersonal attraction. 4. Love. I. Title.
HQ801.T343 2010
306.7--dc22

2009046723

ISBN: 978-1-4019-1854-5

13 12 11 10 6 5 4 3
1st edition, March 2010
3rd edition, June 2010

Printed in the United States of America

For my beloved friend Pat Davidson,
whose dignity, grace, and
courage will always whisper
strength within my soul.

CONTENTS

INTRODUCTION

Ode to a Friend

"Man does not simply exist, but always decides what his existence will be, what he will become in the next moment."

— VIKTOR FRANKL

In the early 1980s, I was introduced to the principles of quantum physics, and the subject became a passion and a guiding force in my life. As a counselor in private psychological practice, I taught my clients how to apply those concepts to their personal experiences—and to shift their consciousness and vibration in order to create much happier lives. I believed then—and I still do—that employing these principles has provided some of the most empowering insights I've ever experienced.

In recent years, however, there has been a lot of confusion about what the laws of attraction are—and how they really work. A wildly simplistic and materialistic viewpoint has expanded, creating a backlash of urgency, fear, and self-blame. An all-or-nothing approach to energy has become so prevalent that people don't know how to interpret the difficult things they go through. They tend to find fault with themselves, which is an extremely unhealthy response. Unfortunately, this only digs them deeper into negativity.

This reaction brings me to my first intention for writing this book: to help you see the laws as tools that can empower you, not as inflexible requirements that you have to fulfill or else you'll be punished. I love these principles, and I hate to think that anyone is using them as just another thing to beat themselves up over.

This is what happened to a dear friend of mine, Pat Davidson, to whom I've dedicated this book. In fact, she's the inspiration that started it all.

About three years ago, Pat was diagnosed with amyotrophic lateral sclerosis (ALS), a progressive condition (also known as Lou Gehrig's disease), which causes people to lose the use of their muscles and eventually become paralyzed. Pat and many of her friends and family had been reading lots of books on attraction, so they began to analyze how she "attracted" this condition and what she did to bring it on herself.

I personally don't believe that her thoughts created this ordeal, although there was a time in her life long ago when she had a lot of fear. She was well past that, however; and she had been leading a happy, purposeful life for decades. In addition, Pat learned that at the time of her diagnosis, there were six other people in her small town who also had ALS, which is a very rare disease. This statistic was way off the charts compared to the national average, so it made me wonder if something environmental was at work. My friend Candace Pert, who's an extraordinary scientist, believes that many of the diseases we see today have links to environmental factors.

Yet at the beginning of her illness, Pat had the tendency to blame herself for contracting the disease; and as time went on, she also blamed herself for not being able to turn it around. She felt there must be something wrong with her if she couldn't use her thoughts to create a miracle; so she tried desperately to visualize, intend healing, and be positive.

This last part was taken to the extreme, however. As her condition intensified, she believed she shouldn't even talk about how she felt. If she told anyone that she was tired or her muscles were weaker, she felt guilty for talking so negatively. Apparently, someone had warned her that if she wanted to get better, she should never admit to feeling bad.

I know this was just well-meaning guidance from loved ones who were determined to do anything to make my friend recover—but it was tough for her. Pat realized that honoring herself was important, however, and she arrived at a new understanding that helped her let go of shame and express her feelings and her experience honestly. Her family and friends became utterly unflinching in their support and dedication to her needs and happiness. Their devotion was an inspiration, as was her love and gratitude for them. In fact, her entire consciousness shifted to love and gratitude, and she was able to totally release her guilt and self-judgment.

Pat and I talked a lot about all of these issues, and it was those discussions that inspired this book. I didn't want anyone else who was going through something so traumatic to compound their troubles with guilt and self-blame. Instead, it would be far better to approach the laws with balanced understanding and to let go of the extremes and the faultfinding.

This is what Part I of this book is devoted to—exploring the common misunderstandings. The nuances may be subtle, but they're very important if you want to retain your power through every type of experience. I imagine that you have some familiarity with the laws of attraction, given their amazing popularity over the past few years. Countless authors have written a vast variety of books dealing with many different aspects of the attraction concept.

I want to say, however, that this book isn't intended to dismiss any theories by other authors. It's only written as a response to my friend's experience—and to the hundreds of e-mails I've received asking for clarification. It's my genuine intention to reduce the all-or-nothing reactions and bring clarity, peace, and balance to all of life's processes, including manifestation and attraction.

Part II is designed to explore the many influences on our destiny creation. This is also a discussion I often had with Pat. If her illness wasn't specifically caused by something in her thoughts, what could be the reason for it? Any number of factors could be an influence, and it's very enlightening to consider them all.

This is my second intention for writing this book—to examine *all* of the elements of attraction and manifestation, and then to see how we can use the power of our consciousness to deal with each one. For example, when we start to understand our soul's higher intentions for this life, we can learn how to align our own personal intentions with that, and create greater fulfillment and greater success in the process.

Also, when we step back and observe life's natural cycles—such as transformation, death, and rebirth—we can learn how to use those passages to bring inestimable growth and enlightenment to both this life experience and to our eternal evolution. When we get a glimpse into our karma and the energetic sources there, we can break old patterns and create new, positive directions for this life and for lifetimes to come.

All of these factors impact our experiences and must be taken into consideration, in addition to the individual factors of personal consciousness, energetic vibration, and intention. Of course, these last three are the starting points of self-actualization and destiny creation, but we must see them through the truth of our eternal and personal reality. This is what Part III is about—establishing an inner reality that reflects the truth of our eternal worth and inestimable power.

Our consciousness is the most important of these personal factors, and our efforts to understand and direct it can turn even the most challenging adversity into a wonderful blessing. But that consciousness must revolve around our true source of power, not the lies of fear and limitation. This is the starting point of our life-force vibration, the core of our creation in personal terms. By establishing a consciousness based in eternal truth, we can more easily influence both the inner and outer factors that are affecting our lives.

Throughout the book, you'll find "*Soul*ution" sections. These are designed to offer techniques and suggestions that address the issues being discussed. Instead of just reading about these ideas, give them a try. The main point of this book is to develop a higher consciousness of all your options in order to see where that self-empowered life force can take you. So consider the responses that come from your heart and soul (thus the spelling—*Soul*ution). This higher viewpoint may be just the change that you need.

To that end, you'll also find suggestions for journaling, with questions and directives in many cases. Don't dismiss these processes; they can bring great clarity and lead you in unknown directions. I've used journaling since my youth, and it has really been a vehicle of personal evolution.

My third intention for writing this book is to encourage you *not* to give up—either in the pursuit of your dreams or in the intention to embrace the power and beauty of the here-and-now. The principles of attraction are very powerful forces, and you can activate them to create an amazing present experience, as well as great results in the future.

You may be frustrated, and if you're not getting the immediate outcomes you desire, you might be tempted to throw out the entire concept of consciousness-created reality. But this principle is far too important to dismiss. Understanding is the key—along with patience and persistence. You'll be moving forward anyway, so you might as well use the power of your consciousness to direct this movement. In fact, your entire life may be designed to lead you to this important choice. Achievements come not merely as a result of focusing on what you want, but more as a result of focusing on your life. The intention to keep progressing on your path—which I refer to often—is a whole-life purpose that's so valuable, it can carry your specific goals with it.

So don't give up on the laws! There are several at play in your life even now. In Chapters 5 and 12, I give an overview of each law, but if you want more information, I explored them all much more thoroughly in my second book, *Quantum Success*. Whatever you do, don't use the wonderful principles of energy and manifestation to find yourself faulty. Instead, love yourself through every experience—and know that when you do, the Universe will listen.

On the cover of this book, you'll find a pool of lotus leaves with their blossoms starting to bloom. The lotus has long been used in Eastern philosophy as a symbol for the blessings that can come from difficulty. From the dark depths of muddy water, a beautiful blossom appears. This is an apt metaphor for the power of consciousness creation. In the depth of difficulty, we can plant the seeds of new beginnings and discover wonderful outcomes getting ready to bloom.

Consciousness is the essence of life, the core of all creation. The more you know, the more you can employ it to break through any difficulty and create amazing benefits. Find out about all the factors that determine your destiny; and when you do; you can bring the power of your consciousness to each one. This moment is the key that unlocks the door. Armed with the truth, you can transform your life and awaken to unexpected blessings and joy.

PART I

The LIES of ATTRACTION

"To find oneself living in an age of doubt is not such a curse. There is a kind of reverence in undertaking the quest for truth, even before the first scrap has been found."

— DEEPAK CHOPRA

CHAPTER ONE

ATTRACTION PHOBIA

"Fear is the main source of superstition, and one of the main sources of cruelty. To conquer fear is the beginning of wisdom."

— BERTRAND RUSSELL

There are forces in the Universe that cannot be denied, and it's bewitching to believe that they can always be controlled and directed at will. It's true that your life force vibrates with vast influence. Consciousness does indeed create reality, and energy expands to produce real and far-reaching results.

These principles are being explored in the scientific world, yet there are still so many things we need to understand—both about our personal energetic process and about the workings of the Universe itself. Truths such as *consciousness-created reality* are fundamental parts of the human experience. And although these concepts are complex, they can empower us and provide many formulas to help us approach life in a healthy and self-actualized way. When we bring our awareness to our everyday experiences, we can not only achieve greater happiness, we can deal with all the joys and difficulties along our path.

Yet there are many misconceptions that have developed around the process of manifestation and attraction. I call them the *lies* of attraction, but it might be more accurate to call them the *half-truths* of attraction. The precepts I'll discuss in the beginning chapters of this book all find their basis in truth, but they lose their integrity—and cause serious problems—when they're taken to the extreme.

For example, the theory of consciousness-created reality does reveal your mental and emotional influence on your own destiny creation. When you hear about this and other concepts that say your thoughts create reality, you may become obsessed with what you're thinking—never realizing that obsession actually makes things worse. This is such a common reaction that it's important to address it right away.

Lie of Attraction

If you want good things to happen to you, you can never allow yourself to have a negative thought.

The *Real* Truth

Negative thoughts are a part of being human. While you certainly don't want to stew in them, you don't want to fear or judge them either. A far greater energy of attraction is letting go, moving on, and not taking things too seriously.

Are you critical of your negativity? Worried about being around people who worry? Afraid of your own fear? This reaction has run rampant. I call it *attraction phobia,* and it's based in the belief that good things only happen to people who *always* think positively. This can be paralyzing because the fear of having a negative thought is, in itself, a negative thought!

A friend of mine was recently going through some very difficult times in her career, suddenly being mistreated and manipulated so that others could try to gain her position. She decided to relax and treat herself to a massage. Her massage therapist was usually very supportive, but had recently been immersing herself in some extreme views of attraction, becoming very judgmental about any "negative" thinking.

It's important to remember, however, that a healthy part of our process as human beings is to express our emotional reactions, especially those concerning the difficulties in our life. My friend had just gotten out of a meeting where she was being attacked, and she naturally felt the need to vent her feelings. She felt that the massage room was a supportive environment—that she was engaging in an activity where she not only could get her thoughts out, but could also get the negative energy out of her body. In addition, her therapist was a long-time confidante, often offering sage advice about challenging situations.

After my friend had been talking about some of the things that had just happened, her massage therapist abruptly stopped her and said, "Well, if you're going to keep complaining, you're never going to attract anything different."

My friend explained that the feelings were still raw, and she was just trying to get them out and understand what had occurred. Yet the therapist became very hostile and judgmental. She told my friend that she should never talk about her difficulties again, and insisted on doing the rest of the massage in silence.

This inflexible, black-and-white approach has become a terribly common and extremely unhealthy reaction. It's not only simplistic, it's unrealistic. It doesn't allow for our humanity, nor does it encourage us to process things in a healthy way.

Real life happens and has to be handled honestly—not superficially. People can be cruel, and if they are, you'll react. Do you want to shelve that response and live in energetic perpetuation, or do you want to let it out and get some resolution? Of course, if you keep running into the same kind of treatment, you do need to investigate how you treat, and talk to, yourself. That's the line of thinking that really matters.

The Thought's the Thing—or Is It?

I like to view some negative thoughts as clouds in the wind. They can float in and out, and you don't have to make them mean too much. Yet if you're like me—and every other human being—there are times when life seems to send huge storm clouds your way. When something truly difficult stimulates a lot of negative thinking, that's a sign you need to deal with it—not ignore it, not deny it, and definitely not fear it.

If you're generally optimistic, minor negative thoughts can move through your mind, but they don't have a lot of power in your life. Chronic patterns of doubt, anger, and self-judgment, however, need to be reversed. Those kinds of thoughts that reappear with frequency and intensity are trying to tell you that you have issues that need attention.

For example, if you're *always* saying, "There are no good men out there," you need to know that such a persistent expectation can set you up for that experience. It also permeates your energy with a sense of hopelessness—certainly not the emotional content you want to be carrying.

Yes, it's true that every single thought and feeling you have will create some energy—even if it's just a moment of joy or an instant of anxiety. But if you do have a flash of fear, does that mean the specific thing you're afraid of will actually manifest? Not necessarily. But it does indicate that negativity in general will move into your consciousness, creating a cloud of agitation that can either grow or decrease depending upon your approach to it. Venting it can actually get it out, while denial can keep it stuck.

Specific thoughts that are repeated—such as fear or appreciation—accumulate in your resonance and determine the quality of your daily life. So it's not necessarily the fleeting ideas that are problematic. It's living in a constant consciousness of fear and judgment that must be changed—because that's what really causes all your misery. Shifting persistent negative patterns will then transform the ongoing emotional quality of your life and generate a real core of happiness in your life-force energy.

We're all human. We all have doubts and worries that seem to come out of the blue. There are some that can just be let go, but others seem to be much more persistent. As we'll explore in Part III, most of the fear and judgment we've learned to live with is *not* our truth. It's up to us to establish a new foundation of positive perception, and that certainly doesn't include constantly fretting.

SOULUTION

Be conscious of your thinking, but have some compassion for yourself. Let the fleeting irritations go, and develop a real awareness about your personal issues. If you notice consistent patterns of negativity, investigate them to find the source of the misinformation. Over time, you can work on changing this and establish consistently healthier mental habits.

You don't have to worry about every single thing you say and think. Keep in mind, however, that the Universe responds most to your core beliefs about yourself. Thoughts of self-love and self-trust are irresistibly magnetic and are really worth your attention!

Word Play

The obsession with always being positive has become so extreme that it has even resulted in rules about what you're allowed to say. In fact, you may have heard the admonition to never use the word *want.* The implication is that it will cause you to focus on the fact that you don't already have your goal. For example, if you say, "I want a man," it only makes you realize that you don't already have one. The theory encourages you to say instead, "I have a wonderful man," and to continue to repeat that until it becomes a reality.

But when it comes to attraction, what you say or how you say it isn't the most important issue. It's your entire life force—the consciousness rooted in your belief system—that really matters. If you're looking for a new relationship, it won't depend on whether you use the words *want* or *have;* it will depend almost exclusively on how you perceive and relate to yourself. You can tell yourself that you *have* a new relationship, and you can put pictures on your treasure map and feng-shui your bedroom with candles and rose quartz; but if you look in the mirror with self-loathing, you're out of luck. It's either not going to happen at all, or you're going to attract a man who's as hateful to you as you are to yourself. The bottom line isn't your words—it's your genuine self-regard and self-care. There's nothing wrong with *wanting* a man as long as you *want* to (and do) love yourself first.

⚖

Lie of Attraction

If you want good things to happen to you, you *must* use correct language and watch everything you say.

The *Real* Truth

When you live from the heart and consistently come from a place of love and honor for yourself and others, it simply won't matter what words you use.

Obsessing about language has just become one more thing for you to beat yourself up about—not an ideal energy in the intention to attract. Some people also say that the word *hope,* like *want,* is just another way to focus on something you don't have. But it's important to understand the power of the subconscious mind. It knows what you do and do not have. You can certainly use the word *have,* but don't discard *hope.* If you refuse to allow hope into your heart, it can dramatically shift your energy and attitude about the future—and not in a good way.

Hope is an important element in the human experience. What would we strive for if we could never allow ourselves to imagine something better? Some people say that the word implies lack, but when I hear it, I feel optimism and a sense of unlimited future potential. Hope has driven people to great inventions and discoveries. It can heal, renew, and provide motivation and emotional sustenance. In fact, living without it causes depression and feelings of resignation and pointlessness. Hope is a key ingredient for happiness, and having something to look forward to inspires strength and enthusiasm.

In good times and bad, genuine hope is a vibrant force that's an intrinsic piece of our motivation to grow and change. It's at the center of our efforts in pursuit of personal awareness and self-mastery. After all, why would we ever work on ourselves if we didn't hope to create a more healthy and joyous life? This concept is also at the center of our efforts for others, for knowledge, for the environment, and for every worthwhile cause.

So instead of striking the word from our vocabulary, we should all make its optimistic energy a part of our daily life. I have hope for my children, the planet, our species, and harmony among all races and cultures. I, for one, will never stop hoping.

Soulution

Live in contentment and appreciation for what you have, and remain ever hopeful for the future. You'll find it's much more exciting to get up in the morning and easier to sleep peacefully through the night. Try the following affirmation, and feel its meaning and energy lift you up: I am happy and hopeful, so grateful, and blessed. My life is full of peace, appreciation, and joyous expectation.

Bizarre Attraction Advice . . . Really?!

I get e-mails and phone calls from people all over the world, telling me their attraction stories. In recent years, I've been getting a slew of requests for feedback from people who have gotten somewhat questionable attraction advice and who want a second opinion. The following stories and suggestions are just a few of the true—but truly unbelievable—stories I've heard.

Vegetable Madness

A woman who had developed a serious illness was told by her nutritionist that she should eat more healthy foods, especially broccoli. But her "attraction coach" said that if she knew she was eating the vegetable because she was sick, it would actually be bad for her and maybe even make her more sick! Instead of viewing her new food choice as self-actualized, her coach turned it into something negative. This is fear based, fatalistic, and just plain foolish.

How's this for an option? Be proud of your new self-actualized choices. Eat the broccoli, drink plenty of water, and do other nurturing things that will help put you in charge of your own healing. As you do, affirm: *I am making healthy choices in all that I eat, think, and do. Every cell in my body is blessed with the vitality and health of Divine consciousness.*

Speaking of Sickness . . .

A friend of mine was experiencing myriad symptoms for which her family doctor was unable to provide a diagnosis. When she went to a specialist, another friend, who had read some books on attraction, warned her not to get too detailed in telling the new physician about her symptoms. He said that would mean she was focusing too much on the negative. He actually advised her not to reveal all of the information to the new doctor who was trying to diagnose her!

She was also told to stop using the word *healing* in her affirmations because that meant she was focusing on being sick. In my opinion, however, getting better is a good thing—far better than the alternative. And whether we're healing ourselves, our relationships, our bodies, or our planet, it's always a wonderful intention to bring love where there may be pain, and light where there may be darkness. That's what healing—and higher intention—is all about, so never fear the word or the process itself.

And if you're dealing with some medical issues, think twice when someone advises you not to get treatment and just use your thoughts instead. Of course your consciousness is capable of miraculous healing, and you should always consider that as one of your most powerful tools. But don't dismiss the valuable medical and alternative approaches. *You* are in charge—use everything your world has to offer.

Fear of Fat

I recently heard a story that related a rather extreme viewpoint. This woman said that because she wanted to stay thin, she never let herself look at fat people. She must believe that even just seeing the image of an overweight person could cause the same thing to happen to her.

In my opinion, this point of view is so fearful and unhealthy that it's difficult to know where to begin. First, it's totally disempowering because it makes the mere sight of others more powerful than your own ability to make healthy choices. You must assume the power in your own life, whether it's about food, drinking, money, or anything else. Second, it reveals an extremely judgmental attitude, making others' appearance more important than their character, integrity, and personal worth. Finally, this approach must severely limit the woman's resources for support, input, and even happiness and fun. There are plenty of individuals who might be overweight; and who are wonderful and valuable in many ways, including friendship, love, and guidance. Personally, I'd much rather spend my time with a heavy person who's loving, genuine, and self-empowered than with a skinny person who's fearful, judgmental, and willing to give her power away.

To Care or Not to Care

About a year ago, I was advised never to tell people to "take care" when I say good-bye. I guess the person thought it was a negative statement implying that one must be watchful because something could go wrong. The meaning—and energy—of the phrase depends on the person who says it, and I imagine that some people do intend it as a warning.

I've never actually considered the salutation to "take care" to be negative. Quite the opposite, in fact. I close phone conversations with it, and I've said it to my clients for years. To me, it's a gentle reminder to prioritize yourself and to look after your own needs. After all, shouldn't we always take care of ourselves? When lovingly spoken, it's wonderful advice.

I Walk the Line

A client once told me that she felt as though she spent all her time "troubleshooting" her thoughts, always analyzing if they were positive or negative, and being upset when they went the wrong way. She told me that her husband had been critical—but she didn't want to talk about her resentment over it. She said, "I know that words create energy, and if I say I have resentment, then that will only increase."

She also wanted to address her weight gain since menopause. When she told me, "I've gained 15 pounds," she also added that she hadn't wanted to say that out loud. When I asked why, she said it was only acknowledging a negative thing.

In both cases, however, she needed to start with what was real in order to deal with the situation. After all, how can you resolve a problem if you don't allow yourself to identify it first? Yes, words do create energy, but the fear of them creates energy, too. Life is real, and difficult things can happen. If you refuse to talk openly and honestly about your experience, you'll only be living in denial, perpetuating the problem, and carrying the resonance of the unresolved situation with you.

⚖

Deal or No Deal

These and many, many other stories have been brought to my attention due to the ever-increasing panic over negative thoughts. It seems that many people have arrived at a zero-tolerance attitude regarding thinking or even feeling bad. A client recently told me, "I spend so much time trying to go to the 'feel-good' place, I don't even recognize what I really think or feel about anything anymore."

But life can often be hard, and if you're a human being—which I assume you are—you're going to have to face your own hurts, losses, or frustrations at some point or another. So don't freak out if you feel bad about them. Both negative and positive emotions are all a part of the human experience. When problems arise, even if they're unpleasant, they must be dealt with. Denying the difficulty doesn't make the problem go away or purify its energy; it only stuffs the vibration deep into your consciousness and tells the Universe that you're unwilling to prioritize yourself and the issues in your life. A healthy approach requires facing the problem, venting your feelings about it, and dealing with the challenges it raises.

⚖

Lie of Attraction

If you want good things to happen, you should never talk about anything bad—or even let yourself have unhappy feelings at all.

The *Real* Truth

You empower yourself by dealing with your history. Purify your energy by venting your emotions, determining what honors you, releasing what doesn't, and then moving on.

This is extremely important: *If you have something uncomfortable going on, the solution is not to shut down—it's to open up.* Whether it's a new hurt or an old trauma, your energy is punctuated by the events in your life. If you've never vented the emotions around the pains of the past or even the difficulties of today, then it becomes impossible to shift your conclusions about those experiences. Over time, the refusal to deal with the vagaries of life will cause you to feel more and more like a victim. You will, however, reclaim your power when you take action to resolve things—and when you express the honest emotions you're experiencing.

When something happens to you—whether it's somebody running into your car or something life changing like losing a relationship or a job—it's normal for you to have anger, fear, and doubts. When the feelings are unexpressed, they stay in your personal energy field and influence your life-force vibration. The unresolved agitation will persist and become a part of your *signature resonance*. But you can release that when you finally acknowledge what you genuinely feel and arrive at some new conclusions.

I often liken this phenomenon to the Pigpen character in the Peanuts cartoons. No matter where he goes, Pigpen carries a cloud of dirt all around him. It's a similar phenomenon with the energy of your pent-up emotions. You may refuse to say, feel, or even think anything negative, but if you have unfinished, unexpressed stuff swimming in your energy field, people are going to pick up on that; and situations that resonate with that vibration are going to be drawn to you. It's very important, therefore, to let yourself get it out. Express your feelings and investigate any false or dishonoring conclusions that the difficult experience may be perpetuating.

SOULUTION

The remedy to all this confusion about negativity is balance. You must express your deeper feelings and intervene on your self-condemning thoughts. The last thing you want to do is attack yourself for your unpleasant emotions or thoughts—that's just digging yourself in deeper. On the other side of the coin, you do want to notice and change repeated negativity, especially self-criticism and hopelessness.

Balance is the key. Ventilate your feelings honestly. Change chronic false assumptions to ones that support your intention to live in self-love and genuine power. Honor your process every step of the way.

Amanda's Process

Amanda came to see me because she was frustrated with her love life. She was a pretty, easygoing woman with a great sense of humor, yet for years she'd been attracting critical or unavailable men. She wanted to find out why and shift her attraction level. Initially, she thought I was going to give her a few affirmations and help her with her treasure map. She felt that would be all she needed to make a difference. Unfortunately, she was mistaken.

When I asked Amanda about her childhood, she told me she didn't want to talk about it. She said her parents provided her with everything she ever needed. Neither one was an alcoholic, nor were they violent. As a result, she couldn't understand how her history could have anything to do with her relationship experiences now.

I told her to humor me, and she proceeded to tell me about her past. Her parents were caring, hardworking people who lived in a middle-class neighborhood. They had very specific beliefs, however, about what was important in life and what made a woman valuable. Among many well-meant but misguided notions, they taught her that without a husband, she could never be secure; and without a family, she could never be happy. In addition, her grandmother was very fearful; and there were many limitations placed upon her understanding of love, life, and her own value.

In hearing Amanda's history, I realized that unconditional love was never modeled for her. Guided by the fears and values of those around her, she attached the expectation of affection to personal perfection. She even confided to me that there were many times when a partner left, and she wondered what was wrong with her—why she wasn't enough to make the man stay.

Although she'd never considered the profound impact of her past, her childhood drama had led her to some serious conclusions that were perpetuating a life force of self-negation. Deep down, Amanda felt she was unworthy of love, even though she was taught that her only value would come from a relationship. She was totally conflicted because she believed she had to be perfect in order to be approved of, and that she had to be approved of in order to be valuable.

Amanda had been feeling this way her entire life, but she'd never understood or articulated it before. Now she knew what had to be changed: her negative self-view and her expectations of dismissal. She was finally willing to let go of the false assumptions of her old story and start living the truth of her unconditional value and deserving. In order to do that, we set up the following three-step process:

1. Vent the unexpressed emotions and energy. Amanda had never dealt with the feelings of pain and confusion that her conditional approval brought her. In many ways, her parents had been very loving, so she hadn't even realized that she was angry about the way her innate value had been minimized when she was a child. She now knew that holding on to that energy was causing excessive striving and self-judgment as an adult. In order to release the negativity, she started writing a series of letters to her mother, father, and grandmother in her journal. She never intended to mail them, so she could vent all of her feelings honestly, without fear.

As she started writing about her past in this unedited way, she was surprised to find many old memories she hadn't thought about in years coming to the surface. She hadn't been aware of the pain, confusion, and negative energy she'd been living with. Nor did she realize that she was capable of having such a response now that she was in her 30s. But she expressed the emotions as they came up; and as she did so, she was able to work on the second step of her process: figuring out the false beliefs she'd formed as a result of this subtle but extremely influential misinformation.

2. Identify and intervene on the resulting false assumptions. Amanda's conditional approval at home taught her to believe some terrible falsehoods. She was living with conclusions that had been forged in the false priorities and old-fashioned stereotypes of parents who were simply incapable of giving her a self-honoring truth. Although she hadn't thought this through before, she now realized that her entire life was based on a lie her childhood assumption that she needed to strive and seek value externally. She'd successfully donned a mask that allowed her to function easily; but it covered up an undercurrent of negative feelings, including unworthiness, inadequacy, and emotional insecurity. Her thoughts were full of self-condemnation and fear of rejection—it was time to move on.

Amanda listed each negative conclusion, identifying it as merely an unhealthy habit that came from a story that simply wasn't true. The list included beliefs such as: *The world is limited, and so am I. There must be something wrong with me. I must be loved by a man to be valuable—but without any value, I don't deserve to be loved.*

At first these thoughts surprised her, because they were in total opposition to the easygoing and carefree persona she'd been presenting to others for years. It turned out she'd been living two lies: the one of her unworthiness and the pretense of having no feelings at all. When she awakened to these false identities, she was finally free to let them go. She continued to vent, identify, and release the unhealthy emotions and inaccurate thoughts as she added the third step to her process of moving on.

3. Establish and integrate a healthy, new belief system based in self-love and truth. Although Amanda's thoughts were full of self-condemnation, she had to introduce new assumptions that represented her truth. She was worthy of love just as she was. She deserved a fully present, caring, and available relationship. She was perfect even in her imperfection, and she deserved to be acknowledged and prioritized—by herself and by others.

All of these thoughts were very foreign to her at first, so we had to open her heart and her life to the truth in ways that her subconscious mind would accept. She started doing affirmations such as: *I am beginning to see how really valuable I am. I am whole and complete just as I am. I deserve to make myself a priority and to expect that from others. I deserve to be loved and to love myself. The world is unlimited, and so am I.*

In this way, Amanda was able to get the old, toxic energies out of her life-force vibration and project a pure, self-loving energy that was far more attractive. As she reversed her old conclusions, she continued to vent the anger and hurt that had been hidden for years. She aggressively worked on living her value and her unconditional truth, and she supported her new understanding with choices of self-care. Her fresh attitude was a real source of joy, and she finally became happy for the first time. Not surprisingly, the choice to create this for herself eventually attracted a wonderful man who truly loved her and wanted to stay.

When the Thought Should Be Fought

This is where the issue of changing your thinking becomes imperative. When you hear yourself judging or condemning yourself, it's a major red flag that your thoughts must be changed. Reversing *consistent patterns* of self-negation is far more important than worrying about fleeting negative ideas or using words such as *hope* or *want* instead of *believe.* It's your self-perception and your self-love that will bring real energetic harmony and guide your life force forward. This core truth not only determines the quality of your life, it also influences the results of your dreams and desires.

Don't obsess over your "attraction language." The most important language is that of self-love. When you're continually using words that don't honor you, then that's the stuff you really need to change. When you recognize the language of the old lies you were taught—phrases such as *I'm a failure, I don't deserve,* and *I don't believe in myself*—take a deep breath and affirm: *I release that. I bless myself and live in the beauty and truth of my eternal worth. I am free. I am deserving, and I am filled with value just as I am.*

A big part of the power of attraction comes from your peace of mind, so don't panic over every negative response. And since no random thought can ruin things for you, don't make yourself crazy scrutinizing every word you think and say. When you recognize a persistent pattern of fear or self-judgment, simply make it your highest priority to change that habit.

The intention to bring healing, trust, and love to your own heart will ignite your life force with brilliant energy. In the deepest understanding of *consciousness-created reality,* it's your pervasive peace and gentle self-care that make your life magnetic. All attraction starts with this truth: You are worthy of your own love.

CHAPTER TWO

THE BLAME GAME

"Experience is not what happens to a man. It is what a man does with what happens to him."

— ALDOUS HUXLEY

Engaging the power of your consciousness can be truly life altering. It will give you strength in times of trouble, solace in times of sorrow, and tools to handle anything that may come up. The potential blessings are unlimited when you live with this understanding, yet the possibility of misery can be equally great when you have a single-minded focus about how attraction works. When all your effort is devoted to creating good, yet something horrible happens, what could be the source?

An unfortunate response is the tendency to blame yourself for your difficulties. It's a widespread misunderstanding that can cause you to become very confused and self-condemning. You may end up looking at all the problems in your life, thinking, *I brought this on myself,* but that's a totally counterproductive interpretation. While it may be necessary to make some personal changes—and it's always helpful to examine the energy in your life—there are also many other influences on the myriad events you encounter.

LIE OF ATTRACTION

If something bad has happened to you or your family, then it must be your fault.

THE *REAL* TRUTH

There are many factors that influence your experiences. If you're in a challenging situation, you can shift your consciousness, but faulting yourself only disempowers you more. You have all the resources you need to understand what's happening and to work on altering your awareness so that you can move out of the difficult cycle.

It's truly self-sabotaging to label yourself a failure—or to engage in self-blame or faultfinding—when you're in a difficult situation. This reaction only buries you in a hole of negativity, which is exactly the pit you're trying to escape. The more unpleasant something is, the more important it is to get out of the blame game and choose the clarity and self-empowerment that will let you move on.

As a counselor, I know how difficult it can be to create a healthy, happy, and consistently positive mindset—especially if you were raised in a home filled with negativity, judgment, or fear. It takes great effort and willingness to change. When a belief system is forged in such conditions, it's all the more important to be patient and self-forgiving. But if you jump into self-criticism and blame with every challenging situation in your life, you're only returning to the source of information that you're trying to clear up. *If you want patterns of difficulty to change, you must change your reaction to them.*

The Gods Must Be Angry

Faulting yourself for the bad stuff deteriorates both your sense of power and your sense of deserving. Many people even feel that they're being punished by God or the Universe—or the cosmic laws themselves—because they've been engaging in some unknown wrongdoing. In fact, some seem to have made a bizarre leap from the impartial laws of attraction to a weird Judeo-Christian mentality of being rewarded for good thoughts and punished for bad.

But the laws *are* impartial; they are *not* punishing you. It's far too simplistic to say that everything difficult comes from your mental makeup. Of course it's true that consciousness creates reality, but many events occur for other reasons. As you'll explore more thoroughly in Part II, factors such as life cycles, spirit cycles, karma, and soul intention all play a part in your personal process. And that's exactly what this life is—your soul's eternal process—and some of its motivations may as yet be unknown to you.

The fact is, there's a lot that has yet to be discovered, both about the world itself and about the human experience. Dark energy and dark matter make up more than 90 percent of the universe, but scientists still don't know what and where they are. Our lives are like that, too. We can certainly understand a lot about how our consciousness and our life force contribute to our personal experiences. These are very important factors, and they should never be dismissed. But sometimes unexpected things can happen, and we may not yet know why.

One thing is certain: blaming yourself only makes you feel faulty and miserable. That life force of misery—if you persist in it—will eventually beget more of the same. So is self-blame really the response you want to engage in when you're trying to get out of the morass?

Both self-condemnation and assumptions of punishment are amazingly skewed and dangerous reactions to the principle of consciousness-created reality. The resulting fear and self-loathing create such a paralysis of thought and action that it's impossible to see the truth—not only about the source of the problem, but also about what to do next.

Soulution

A combination of a self-loving attitude along with peaceful action is much more productive than lingering in self-blame, and fear of Universal punishment. This is true no matter what type of difficult situation you may be facing—whether it concerns your career, your finances, your love life, your health, or any other issue.

Investigate your thinking to see how you can approach the situation with honor and self-empowerment, but let the blame go. Your choice to move forward with optimism and action will bring healing to the problem and to your reaction.

In Sickness and in Health

One of the most difficult things to understand concerning the laws of attraction is why certain people get sick—and if they've created it themselves. It's especially hard to understand why children become ill. How can they create conditions such as leukemia or autism from their innocent thinking? For that matter, how can an adult who's optimistic and self-loving suddenly get sick and die? Unfortunately, there's a New Age mentality that says: "If you're sick, your thoughts created the disease." And as if that's not enough, some people actually double the guilt by declaring, "If you really wanted to, you could get better."

Needless to say, I truly have faith in the power of belief and consciousness. I've been teaching these principles for decades, and I'll be the first to say that they can change reality right down to the cellular level. Miracles can happen at any moment—we must never lose sight of that! And while always being open to receiving a miracle, we need to realize that we may not always know all of the causes of, or solutions to, an illness.

I recently saw a talk show where a New Age author was asked about the power of thought and illness. Her response was that everybody should be able to cure their own cancer. Although I felt certain this person intended this statement as a form of encouragement, I couldn't help but think of all the people watching who were having a hard time dealing with a life-threatening illness and were now wondering what was wrong with them if they just couldn't effect a healing.

A similar thing happened to my dear brother-in-law Rudy when he was in the last months of fighting his battle with colon cancer. Someone actually told him, "You must want to die, or you'd be able to get better." I know this person was only coming from desperation and grief; but that kind of attitude is not only hurtful and judgmental, it's just plain wrong.

Telling people they *should* be able to heal themselves may seem like encouragement, but it can really be unkind because it finds them faulty at a time when they're most vulnerable. Not only that, it actually reverses the energy of healing. I remember Rudy often asking, "What's wrong with me? I do the meditations and the affirmations, and I'm not getting better. I *should* be able to do this." This type of self-judgment certainly won't create relaxation and self-love.

After years in psychology, I can tell you how we respond to *should* statements—especially those that we're unable to fulfill. As children we often hear admonitions such as: "You should be more like your brother," "You should get better grades," and "You should never cry or show weakness." We hear these *shoulds* and use them as evidence of our own inadequacy, an ever-present reminder of our inability to achieve the expected results.

Even as adults, the *shoulds* in our lives cause us to create attitudes of striving and desperation; and if we're unable to perform, they result in a profound sense of unworthiness. All of these reactions are extremely toxic energetic vibrations. In terms of attraction, that poisonous resonance is guaranteed to sabotage our quality of life; and the energy of striving strictly counters the intention of success—in healing or anything else.

As a proponent of the power of personal consciousness and energy, it pains my heart to know that those who are living with a difficult disease are using these principles to make themselves feel worse. First, they find themselves faulty because they contracted the diseases in the first place; then they feel like even bigger failures because they haven't been able to heal themselves through their thinking.

It's true that belief and emotion can be linked to sickness, but blaming yourself for getting ill or for not having healed yet is totally self-defeating. Of course, you could investigate whether or not there are any cognitive or emotional changes that you could make. Studies have shown that cancer occurs at a higher rate among people who are passive or depressed. Arthritis has been linked to unexpressed emotions. But keep in mind that both of these diseases—and many more—also run in families and have connections to diet, smoking, pesticides, and other environmental factors. So instead of blaming yourself, it's far better to *love* yourself through it.

SOULUTION

If you want a healthier body, it's always a good idea to create healthier mental and emotional habits in your life. Do what's necessary to change patterns such as depression, anxiety, or the inability to speak your truth. Honor yourself both in your thoughts and your physical choices. Making self-honoring the basis of your daily decisions is one of the best things you can do to heal on all levels.

A shift in consciousness can happen in the blink of an eye, and a miraculous healing can take place at any moment. No matter what you're going through, you can always charge your thoughts with hope, faith, and optimism. Instead of finding yourself faulty, reclaim your power, and always take action on your own behalf. Allow yourself to use every healthy approach at your disposal to help you deal with the difficulty at hand. And never forget that spirit is with you and willing to help.

Beware of the admonition to "heal yourself *only* through your thinking." This attitude has encouraged some individuals to ignore much-needed medical treatment and even alternative healing techniques as well. Someone told me once that she was advised not to "do" anything because "working on healing" meant admitting to being unwell! This type of fear and denial frightens me. You wouldn't refuse to get a cast on a broken leg just so you could *think* the bones into wholeness and healing. Why would you dismiss treatment for something more serious?

You don't have to define yourself by your disease in order to work on making it better. So get advice, advocate for yourself, and weigh all the information. Do what you need to do in order to honor and nurture yourself. Take responsibility for directing your thoughts in a more positive way, but release the self-blame that makes you feel faulty and afraid. Charge your life force with this intention: *I am strong and capable of handling anything that may come my way. I am self-loving, and I always take action on my own behalf. I am whole, healthy, eternal, safe, and wise.*

The Soul of a Child

If individual consciousness creates reality, how can an innocent child suffer from things such as disease, pestilence, and starvation? This question evades a logical answer when we limit our perception of this world to a strict interpretation of the laws of attraction alone. There's a lot more going on than we may know, yet there are some people who are very quick to pass judgment on this point.

One of those individuals was on a national radio show discussing a recent event where a six-year-old girl was kidnapped and murdered. The host asked his guest how something like that could happen where the laws of attraction were concerned. Unbelievably, the guest actually replied, "It's the parents' fault." He went on to say that since a child didn't have an adult consciousness it must be the adults' thoughts and energy that created the reality.

This response was so horrific—and inaccurate—that it rendered me speechless in the moment. I couldn't imagine the pain it would bring to parents who had either lost a child or were in the midst of seeing one suffer.

In fact, after that broadcast, I received hundreds of e-mails from distraught parents saying things such as: "My child has leukemia; what did I do to create it?" and "My son has autism; how did I *think* that into being if I never really thought about it before?"

Not only did these moms and dads have to face the terrible ordeal of watching their beloved children suffer, they were now doubling their pain by taking on the guilt of causing the situation. The self-recrimination and utter confusion were clear. But what remained unclear was what they could do to change their perceptions and arrive at a place of peace in spite of it all.

Let me set the record straight. If your child is going through some difficulty, it's only your fault if you're the one being negligent or doing harm—or if you knowingly allow someone else to do so. If you're being hurtful, critical, absent, or neglectful in your child's care and emotional support, then you need to change things and start making your son or daughter a genuine priority. But if your child is suffering from an illness or condition that has nothing to do with your treatment—or if, God forbid, something terribly tragic happens outside of your control—it's not the "fault" of your thinking or consciousness.

Such profoundly intimate relationships as parent and child or husband and wife are a phenomenon of shared consciousness. Your soul and the souls of those who are close to you have decided to come together in this life in order to achieve something. Whether it's to learn a lesson, to express love in a new and wonderful way, or to process an old energy that may be lingering from previous existences, your time here together has a spiritual purpose. It's important to know this in order to give both your relationships and the experiences within them deeper meaning. This is especially true when the journey includes suffering and loss.

The Spirit's Point of View

The soul follows many paths in this world, varying from sublime peace to great agitation, from wild excitement to profound pain. Any one of these may be a part of the lessons your spirit pursues. As you'll see, there are many life cycles, as well as cycles of learning. In fact, sometimes an entire lifetime is devoted to learning. As a result, it's important to be open to the messages you're given within the situations around you.

There's a purpose in every part of your spirit's process. It's encoded in your consciousness and in the experiences themselves. Part of it is to see a higher value, to find something of greater significance in both the good and the bad. Perhaps the difficulties you encounter are meant to send you on this search, directing you to start seeking a deeper meaning for your spiritual path—and for your life itself.

Your spirit has a vastly different point of view. The soul doesn't mind if the body is sick because it sees life eternally. It remains undaunted by the problems you face, no matter how severe. When steeped in suffering, however, that's all the personality can see. It's similar to the child who feels he's suffering because he has to wear braces. However, like the soul, the parent sees the larger truth and knows that the pain is short-lived—and the benefits worthwhile.

And what might those benefits be? Always, always, the soul seeks love, understanding, unity, truth, and Source. As difficult or as joyous as an experience may be, if it leads you in those directions, the value is great.

The peace of walking—and trusting—in spirit is a vital lesson to learn. Your soul wants you to see yourself as eternal, courageous, strong, and resilient; and it wants you to know that you're always supported and adored. To choose love for yourself, to arrive at a higher purpose and a clearer understanding—these are lessons that your soul longs for you to embrace. And these are the truths it sings in your heart: *I am powerful. I am eternal and free—from worry, limitation, and fear. I am Divine; I am alive with Divine light. I am spirit. I am love. I am peace.* Affirm these truths often, for they are at the heart of your reality, guiding you in good times and bad.

Time After Time

In my own life, I've been gifted with some pretty miserable situations. In fact, my most valuable lessons were given to me as a result of some of my most challenging experiences. When my father died in a car accident, I didn't think I was ever going to get over it. I didn't realize it at the time, but I felt abandoned; and deep inside, I was angry at my father for leaving. Since I couldn't accept his death, I certainly couldn't express my emotions about it. Not knowing what else to do, I internalized all my pain and rage.

That was a big mistake. Within two years, I developed chronic respiratory infections. I had several bouts of pneumonia and suffered what seemed to be incurable bronchitis for nearly two more years. Eventually, I found out I'd developed hypogammaglobulin anemia. It seems that my inability to deal with my father's death had depleted my immune system and given me a condition that I've been receiving transfusions for over the last 20 years.

So what really *is* the source of this disease in my life? Is it my fault that I developed this condition? Did I *think* myself sick? For that matter, did my own consciousness cause my father's car accident?

I could make myself crazy trying to figure out all the hows and whys, but there's one thing I know for sure: as difficult as my father's death (and absence) has been, processing that experience, along with the illness that followed, has brought me profoundly valuable gifts.

The first was a deeper understanding of consciousness, readiness, and capability. Sometimes the choices we make are uninformed and may even be downright unhealthy. Perhaps we even make serious mistakes; but it's possible that, given the circumstances, it was all we could have done at the time.

This was the case when I couldn't grieve for my father. In spite of the fact that I was a counselor at the time, I simply had no personal readiness to mourn a loss of that depth. I could have—and should have—sought therapy to get it all out. I didn't, however; and I ended up internalizing everything, sending it deep into my body instead of getting it out.

Could it be that this decision made me sick? Yes, it certainly could. But it would have been pointless for me to fault myself. Instead, I had the choice to love myself through it. When I finally did realize the error of my denial, however, I opened myself to the pain and let it all come out. I was able to deal with it and arrive on the other side with a far greater awareness of how I needed to change my approach to life. The process was a huge shift in consciousness for me, a great gift in the grief.

That experience gave me the skills and strength that I was able to carry forward. It was brought home to me in no uncertain terms that as human beings, we absolutely need to identify and vent our pain, sorrow, and anger. Ever since that time, I've kept up my own process of journaling in order to get toxic energies and feelings out of my body and mind. I've also been able to teach others the necessity of identifying and expressing their emotions, and many have found it a helpful and even life-changing skill.

This is more valuable than I can say, and I want to go on record as stating that journaling is one of the most empowering things I've done to change my thinking and develop clarity about the situations I've been in. In addition to being a simple technique for expressing highly charged feelings, it's also been a very worthwhile tool in analyzing the direction of my thoughts and coming to new conclusions. It has helped me increase my level of gratitude, analyze my options, and shift my consciousness to a much more peaceful resonance.

That long-ago experience was so unpleasant—with respect to both the loss of my father and in the following years of illness—that there were times I thought I'd never get through it. In fact, at one point I was so sick that I actually had a full-blown near-death experience. It was one of the most frightening and enlightening blessings of my life, and it never would have happened if I hadn't been so terribly ill.

I learned other things during that period—such as how to speak my truth and the importance of embracing my unique identity. The value of these and all the other lessons of that time is inestimable, but the most rewarding gift of the entire experience was that it brought me closer to spirit. I meditated more, I wrote more, and I learned how to find a more meaningful peace. All of that brought me to a deeper level of faith than I'd ever had before.

It's ironic, because when my father passed away, my initial reaction was that my beliefs had been shaken to the core, and I didn't think I could ever trust in anything again. Yet I now know that those hard times gave me strength and moved my life forward in amazing ways.

SOULUTION

If you or a loved one is going through a difficult time, don't deny it. Your denial may make you feel better on the surface, but pretending the problem or grief doesn't exist will only send the poisonous energy deeper inside. So let yourself feel the raw, open emotions that come to the surface. Move into them and really allow yourself to experience the hurt, anger, or fear. Scream, cry, or pound it out. Vent the feelings in your journal and express them to loved ones—or professionals—who will be supportive. Get it all out so that you can move on.

The choice to let go of guilt and self-blame is an important step in reversing difficulties—no matter what the source may be. Instead of condemning yourself for the problem, ask your spirit what you're meant to learn, or perhaps what you're meant to change. Even if the trouble is coming from within, it's not "wrong," but just a habit that you may need to alter. Investigate what you can do now to gently shift your thinking to increased trust and love. Remember that you always have the option to see your eternal value and truth. As difficult as it may seem, filling your consciousness with self-compassion is the first step in finding the gifts in your grief. Of course you don't need to suffer in order to learn, but if challenges arise, it's likely there's a lesson in them.

Can't See It, Can't Feel It—
What the Hell Is Wrong With Me?

In addition to faulting yourself for the bad, there's another form of the blame game that you might get caught up in, concerning attraction: blaming yourself for the fact that you can't seem to make something good happen. This can result in a lot of fear and guilt. You may think you have to "feel it to achieve it," but when you can't create the emotion or the outcome you want, you may feel hopeless.

Lie of Attraction

You must believe in the end result and feel as though it's already happened. If not, your failure in thinking means that nothing good will ever happen to you.

The *Real* Truth

You'll never be a failure at thinking if you live from your heart. Good things happen even when you least expect them. All you have to do is plant the seed, let go, be patient, and live in peace and self-love.

Recently, a client came to my office in tears, proclaiming that she was a failure. I asked her what was wrong and what she'd tried to do that she found so difficult. She told me she'd been listening to a CD on attraction; and the lecturer had said that when she did her visualizations and affirmations, she must feel the sensations of excitement that come with the completion of her goals. The lecturer went on to say that only by feeling as though she'd already achieved her dreams would she give those intentions enough energy to make them happen.

She sobbed as she said, "My goals are to get a job and find a relationship. But I haven't worked in 3 years, and I haven't had a real relationship in 20. So when I sit there and affirm it and try to believe it, I just can't feel it in my heart—and if I'm such a failure in my thinking, how can I ever succeed in making those goals come true?"

But her lack of feeling wasn't her fault. Your subconscious mind resists believing the polar opposite of your experience. After all, if you know in your heart that something isn't currently a reality—and hasn't been for quite a while—your subconscious won't know how to reconcile the difference.

Again, this isn't something you should blame yourself for—it's a simple issue you can work around. Although having the *feeling* of an experience is a great energizer, many people accomplish phenomenal things with life force, hope, and intention. After my second divorce, I didn't really believe a stable man existed, but I figured I'd be dating, so I put my intention out there and focused on creating a happy and fulfilling life for myself. I may not have believed, but I opened my heart to the possibility. And although I was in no hurry, I met my husband soon after.

SOULUTION

Let go of the self-blame, and introduce some new conclusions in ways that your subconscious mind will start to accept. Open yourself to fresh possibilities and shift to feelings of hope. Modify your affirmations to make both your subconscious mind and your heart more receptive to the potential outcomes you desire.

I once got a call from a man who was unemployed and living in his father's basement. He was driving a beat-up old car that had a rotting, rusting floor. As he was driving around looking for work, he was listening to tapes on attraction. They told him to shout out, "I'm a millionaire! I believe I'm a millionaire! I'm a millionaire!"

He told me that he consistently did these affirmations with enthusiasm. One time he got so excited about it that he stomped his foot, and his shoe went through the floorboard of his car. His response to that was self-chastising: "Who do I think I'm kidding? I'm an unemployed loser, living in my father's basement, driving a car that has no floor."

He called me, asking, "What's the truth? Is it true that if I just keep saying these things, they'll occur?"

I told him that if he wasn't capable of entertaining the truth of those extreme thoughts in his present circumstances, then it might be difficult to make them happen. Instead, I suggested that he start to introduce enriching thoughts that weren't so opposed to his present circumstances. I gave him affirmations such as: *I am attracting more and more abundance in wonderful and unexpected ways. I open my heart to receiving many new blessings, including a new car and a place of my own. I open my life to increasing wealth, and I am willing to take more action and extend myself in new directions.*

I asked him if these were statements that resonated with him—and which his mind could accept. He said yes, and he was able to say them with a stronger feeling in his heart and far greater peace of mind. It took a while, but he kept taking action and applying for jobs. Over time, he found work and was able to afford his own place and a new car.

Resonating with Your Heart

I get e-mails from people all over the world, asking how they should talk to themselves, what and how they should visualize, and what they should affirm. Many of them are coming from a place of frustration, so they often include the question: "What am I doing wrong?"

Visualization and affirmation are key issues. These individuals have been told that if they picture the end result with just the right amount of detail and emotion, they should be able to achieve it. They've also been told to do their affirmations with feeling; and there are some other very specific rules about affirmations, including never using a negative and always affirming in the present tense. This advice is all well and good if you remember three things:

1. Don't let your intentions become desperate or obsessed with the end results.

2. Choose affirmations and visualizations that resonate with your heart.

3. Affirm and appreciate the value of yourself and your life already.

Soulution

Try not to worry so much about how you word your affirmations. Instead, use statements that empower and honor you and make you feel hopeful. Experiment, introducing changes and outcomes that really resonate in your heart of hearts.

It's actually more important that you affirm yourself rather than your results. Assert your own value and worthiness. Declare that you deserve and are attracting wonderful things, and that every moment and experience of your life brings you something of value. Your eternal spirit contains unlimited wisdom, clarity, peace, and inspiration. Know that you have the ability to create happiness and fulfillment for yourself, then support that intention in your daily choices.

Affirmations are tools that I've used every day for decades. They're so valuable that I feel they've changed the very way I experience and perceive life. I encourage the use of affirmations unreservedly as a lifestyle activity. It's far better to *affirm* yourself than blame yourself, so let the self-judgment go.

Throw away the rules and listen to your heart. Build a momentum based in self-worth and positive perception. Jot down your affirmative options and read them often. Open yourself to joy, peace, and unconditional self-acceptance. You *are* worthy, and you *are* powerful. Whether you feel it now or not, your eternal spirit makes it so.

CHAPTER THREE

FOCUS—HOCUS-POCUS!

"The seeker of the Beloved finds Him through a quiet stillness, not in frantic activity. That search is the purpose of life."

— SARMAD

Most people don't realize that the laws of attraction have been examined for years. You can find discussions on this subject in ancient texts and modern titles that date back to the mid-19th century, and many of those books offer sage advice on how to use certain principles to make your life better. There is unending value in understanding how to raise your vibration, as well as great joy and self-mastery in creating a clarity of consciousness in all you do.

Unfortunately, many individuals have misconstrued the design of these principles recently, narrowing their application to specific plans and goals. But life isn't only about making money or owning nice things, and the energy of the world has a far broader purpose. Limiting your viewpoint will actually reduce the profound power that energy and consciousness can bring to your daily life—not only for results in the future, but for immediate change in the very quality and texture of your day-to-day experiences.

Magic or Misunderstanding?

There's a general belief that the process of attraction is a solitary pursuit, a single approach with no variations. This dangerous assumption can actually lead you in the opposite direction of the goals you seek—largely because the absolute, all-or-nothing attitude creates a toxic energy that can completely reverse your results.

Many people are frustrated, and maybe you are, too. Hearing the success stories of others, you can't understand why the laws don't seem to be working in your life. You might be missing some of the finer nuances of the process, getting stuck in anxiety and single-minded intention, actually digging yourself deeper into the energy of resistance. And your intense reactions could create an ongoing quest for magical and immediate results.

When this happens, the laws of attraction just become another thing for you to feel bad about. It's not apparent that the loss of power comes from focusing on specific things and future events rather than using your energy to live a valued and valuable life. This switches your life-force vibration. Ironically, constantly thinking about the outcome often causes you to lose your peace in the process, a vital element in creating the positive core resonance needed for dynamic destiny creation. This is just one of the common dilemmas you can take a closer look at in order to understand how and why you manifest what you do.

Lie of Attraction

There's only one source of your destiny creation, and that's thinking about your specific intentions.

The *Real* Truth

Although your thoughts are major generators of the quality of your life, not everything you experience is a result of your focused intentions.

Thought and consciousness are truly powerful forces in the Universe. There's no doubt that the thoughts you weave and the beliefs you embrace throughout your life form the basis for all your emotional experiences. These mental interpretations can make you happy or sad, hopeful or depressed, peaceful or conflicted. In this way, your thoughts are a big part of your consciousness creation—sending your self-view, your deeply held beliefs, and your expectations out into the world. But it's the general nature of these conscious experiences that really holds sway over your future.

Soulution

Your life force is driven by your predominant mental patterns and emotional responses. As a result, it will always be a significant part of your journey to gain mastery over your thoughts. Thinking only about what you want, however, can actually distract you from important improvements in your thought process. In terms of your attraction and happiness, there are three mental techniques that are far more important than focusing on your desires:

- *Identifying and gently releasing the negative*
- *Engaging in loving and encouraging self-perceptions*
- *Formulating abundantly optimistic worldviews*

These positive choices are huge factors in your life experience, but it's important to keep in mind that a number of other elements also help forge your future. Some are related to your cognitions, yet others are more mysterious and less predictable. Increased power comes from knowing how to deal with the various influences. Your consciousness plants many of the energetic seeds that you'll harvest in the future; yet factors such as environment, life cycles, shared consciousness, the soul's intention, and karma can also significantly impact the personal, professional, and physical experiences you manifest in this life.

These important elements will be closely examined in Part II of this book, but it's helpful to clear up this fundamental misunderstanding right away. Realizing that the future is influenced by more than just your thoughts can create an increasingly balanced approach to both your present process and your future goals. So let's take a look at some cases of manifestation to find out if specific intentions really have that power. You may be surprised to find that the answer is yes . . . and no.

Source and Serendipity

Can we trace a thought to an outcome? Yes, of course. I can cite many wonderful stories from my own life—and from the lives of my clients and friends—where a clear, positive intention was formulated and beneficial results followed suit.

My good friend, author Peggy McColl, recently told me such a story about selling her home. When she decided to put it on the market, she was told not to expect much activity; the economy was slow and nothing was moving. She was determined—although not desperate—and she wrote her intention down exactly as she desired. She did this in the form of a statement of appreciation, saying: *Thank you, Universe, for selling my home quickly and for the price I want.* In addition, Peggy sought assistance from spirit by asking her mother, who had recently passed on, to help move things along. She also didn't obsess about it; she just gave the task to a Realtor and let it go.

In a relatively short period of time, Peggy got the results exactly as she'd intended. She soon felt a genuine appreciation for the accomplishment: her home sold quickly and for exactly the price she wanted. In this case, the outcome clearly connected to the originating thought.

Yet should she have faulted herself if her home *hadn't* sold? Did those who were unable to sell property in the same neighborhood do something wrong? Perhaps they didn't have strong enough intentions or positive beliefs. Maybe they made tactical mistakes in areas such as staging or pricing. That's entirely possible, but any number of other influences could have also helped or hindered eventual results.

Additional factors may have made Peggy's experience different. Perhaps her mother did her part in connecting the buyer and the seller in the energetic realm. And maybe there were other lessons that the nonsellers had yet to learn—whether about thoughts, intentions, patience, surrender, or even technicalities. Whatever the results, there's usually something to learn.

In fact, there's a lesson for everyone in this story. First, set your intention and support it as best you can with your entire life energy. Live in appreciation, and be aware of (but not obsessed with) your thoughts—not only around the issue, but also in your daily life. Remember to ask for spirit's help and surrender the outcome with patience and trust.

Peggy did all of this and more, and she was able to achieve the results she desired. This is clearly a circumstance where factors of daily life force, intention, and even spirit all came together to move a desire from the energetic realm into personal reality.

But does this mean that you can follow every beneficial event back to an originating thought? Sometimes you have a clear idea of where a positive outcome came from, and you can trace it from beginning to end. Yet there are other times—good and bad—when you'll have no idea why or how a certain result came into being.

I recall a story of how actor Robert Mitchum started his career in theater. (For younger readers who may not be familiar with the name, Johnny Depp refers to Mitchum as one of his favorites.) This popular actor starred in movies and later in television shows from the 1940s through the '90s; and although his career flourished, he came upon it quite by accident.

He left home as a young teenager, looking for adventure, crisscrossing the country on freight trains, making money in odd jobs, and exploring whatever part of America caught his fancy. At one point, he found himself in California, living with his sister, who was trying out for a play. When she asked him to give her a ride to the audition, it changed his life.

She didn't get the part, but the director needed someone for a male role and asked Mitchum, who was sitting in the back of the theater, to read for it. He offered Mitchum the part, and since the teen didn't have a job, he decided to take it—even though he'd never acted or even considered it before.

During the run of the play, he was noticed by a talent agent, who signed him up for a studio contract. Thus began an illustrious career that spanned more than 40 years, yet it all happened with absolutely no forethought or apparent intention. Later, Mitchum said that due to his lack of formal training, he was surprised by his success and very appreciative to have fallen into such a rewarding profession.

So what does this story tell you about cause and effect? It doesn't seem that there was a direct cause connecting Mitchum's thinking to the outcome of his career, but the truth about attraction is that some causes precede the thinking. You may set things in motion, or they may come out of the blue. And there are times when your spirit has something entirely different in mind for you than you may realize.

These are just some of the mysteries of creation you'll read about in the next section, but for now it's important to remember that the best approach is one of open flexibility. Continue to put your intentions out there, but always be open to the unexpected blessings—and lessons—that may come your way.

This balanced approach is what ignites the power of your consciousness creation the most. *Your intention is accelerated when you focus as much on creating a high-quality life right now as you do on your goals.* Your life is happening each and every day, so what you do in this moment is what really counts. Do you intend to engage in happiness, action, and positive attitudes about what's going on now? The truth is that present focus is more likely to lead to success than merely dwelling on potential future gains.

Lie of Attraction

All you have to do is keep focusing on what you want, and eventually it will happen.

The *Real* Truth

Making clear intentions is just one of several attraction factors, including the multidimensional life force created by who you are and what you do every day.

It's your *entire* life force—not just your surface intentions—that will determine the results you attract. This is a far more holistic approach than most people ever think about. Your consciousness is like a hologram, projecting a three-dimensional image of yourself. This vital information field includes your thoughts, beliefs, emotions, attitudes, and physicality. And just as important, it also includes the very core and center of your identity, your soul or spirit. Don't dismiss this crucial and powerful expression of yourself. This rejection of spirit not only dishonors you, it disintegrates your life-force energy and moves you out of Universal flow. It's your holographic representation, from the core of your spirit to the current of your daily life, that matters most.

Soulution

Integrate all the powers of intention, belief, and spiritual centering. This will help you gain momentum in your everyday life, as well as accelerate your individual intentions.

It will also be important to see attraction as merely a part of your life's process, not your sole consideration. Start with a passionate pursuit, release past belief patterns that keep you unhappy, and center your consciousness in the peace and power of your eternal truth.

By living with a real sense of value and purpose in the present moment, you'll raise your life experience to such a dynamic resonance of joy that the outcomes won't matter. Surprisingly, it's at this point that your life force will shine so brightly that you're much more likely to attract your desires anyway.

Faulty Focus

While it's true that knowing what you want creates an energetic direction in your life, the suggestion that you *excessively* visualize the outcome can lead you into dangerous territory. It's somewhat ironic when people say that thinking about what you want will stop you from dwelling on what's missing. The truth is, your constant imagining of the desired results can actually create an approach that's full of lack.

Excessive focus on what you want can energetically reduce the likelihood of getting it. In fact, obsessive outcome orientation can create lack in five important areas:

1. Lack of Flexibility
2. Lack of Receptivity
3. Lack of Action
4. Lack of Surrender
5. Lack of Appreciation

Let's look at each of these elements and see how obsessing about your future desires can actually move you deeper and deeper into want.

1. Lack of Flexibility

Flexibility is a key ingredient to success. While it's necessary to know what you want and be specific in your goals and plans, it's also vital to be flexible in your approach. In fact, it's absolutely crucial that you at least occasionally review all the pieces of your process. You may even need to reconsider and change the ultimate goal itself.

The intention to be flexible requires you to open your mind to *all* of your options, investigate different paths, and welcome spirit's inspiration. You'll need to be willing to make changes—in your plans, and even in your dreams and life direction.

Never forget that the world is abundant, and there are many paths to fulfillment and happiness. When you're looking for a love relationship, it's never just *one* person who can fit the bill. There's also never just *one* way to make money—never only a single career that can be fulfilling and financially rewarding. When you become determined to make only one thing happen, you lose your ability to see the many options all around you.

This refusal to open your mind and heart will block your creativity and productivity—not only in the area you're working in, but in every part of your life. It attracts stagnation and resistance to Universal flow. It also blocks potential blessings and inspiration from the Universe, which is the next type of lack that obsessive focus can bring about.

2. Lack of Receptivity

When you stop *yourself* from being flexible, you also stop the Universe from being flexible. Your choice to narrow your focus can shut down your receptivity to unknown wonders and possibilities. You may feel absolutely certain about what or whom you ultimately desire, but the Universe might have something different in mind. There may be an entirely different—yet equally rewarding—outcome, but your obsession with only one desire can actually create resistance that won't allow *anything* wonderful to come through.

Instead of locking on and potentially losing out, try the following affirmations. Make them real intentions for yourself. As you say them, meditate on their truth and open your heart to higher possibilities.

- *The Universe is abundant, and there are many ways to experience happiness. In fact, I have the power to create joy every day of my life.*

- *I open my heart—and my mind—to the many different blessings and options that the Universe can provide. I am willing, free, and receptive.*

- *Inspiration guides me every day, bringing the insight I need to adjust my outlook. I am flexible, inspired, and open to change.*

Give yourself permission to receive something new, something different from anything you may have ever considered. If you don't, you could be shutting down all of your options completely. As you'll see in the next section, sometimes things just aren't meant to be. In some cases, it's the Universe protecting you; in others, it's your soul nudging you in a different direction. Depending upon these and other variables—such as the cycle you're in or your soul's intention—you may not get that one particular person or job this time around. However, you might receive something even better if you just let go and let the options flow. There could be a wonderful, unexpected lover right around the corner, or the unknown but perfect career just down the road. So create a peaceful, persistent, yet flexible approach. Set your intention for happiness now, and allow the Universe to bring the emotional result you're looking for—even if it's wrapped in a different package. And don't forget to take action daily so that your desires don't remain mere pictures in your mind.

3. Lack of Action

Another dangerous by-product of only focusing on the outcome is that it can destroy the element of action. You may become so obsessed with merely visualizing the end results that you don't build the energetic momentum necessary to make them come true. Of course, you need to be receptive and allow spirit to works its wonders, but you also have to take action in order to show the Universe you're serious about your intent. Even if that activity doesn't result in the specific goal you had planned, it builds an accelerated frequency that propels the general intention of achievement and success forward in your life.

But if you're only focused on the future outcome, it can disconnect you from today's activity and present purpose. This split in attention fragments your energy and slows your momentum. In the long run, it can reduce the direction and fulfillment of your daily pursuits, creating a major energy drain on your whole life force.

For this reason, it's hugely important to pick a goal where you can be as enthusiastic about the process as you are about the outcome. If you really put your heart into the tasks involved, you're much more likely to make it all the way. But if you don't feel that you can enjoy the daily action necessary to achieve your desire, you may need to rethink both the goal itself and the steps needed to get there.

SOULUTION

It's fine to visualize the end results; picture yourself in the desired outcome with all its vivid details. Just as important, however, is imagining your daily activity with enthusiasm. In other words, get up in the morning and ask yourself, What action am I going to take today? Then visualize yourself joyously involved in those activities. See yourself going through your day with energy and excitement.

Do this for a few minutes each morning—and if you can, take a little break in the afternoon to renew your intention for happiness in the process. Picture yourself taking the action, making the sales calls, running the meeting, or working on the project with joy. This activates your energy with present appreciation—not just assigning the potential for gratitude to some unaccomplished future event.

Without focused action, your life becomes a void, but purposeful activity aligns your daily energy with your future plans. Intention without action equals subtraction—actually reducing the power in your life. But intention *plus* action equals attraction—bringing more and more value each and every day. Present focus is also accelerated when you surrender the future with trust.

4. Lack of Surrender

Another problem with goal obsession is that it can make you urgent, desperate, and depressed—a definite problem where attraction is concerned. Your belief that only one outcome can make you happy creates a needy, toxic energy that poisons your life force with unhappiness. Your excessive focus makes it impossible to move into a peaceful place of surrender, which is essential if you truly want to create the energy of calm and trusting expectation.

It's enticing but fraudulent to think that you can control every experience in the future. And, as you'll see in the next chapter, that kind of desperate intention can actually destroy your desires. Instead, you must live fully in the present, continuing to move forward while letting go of the need for control. *Surrendering attachment is essential for authenticity and true happiness, two vital energies in the search for success.*

In fact, the ability to live with joy in spite of uncertainty is one of life's big lessons. In addition, the choice to let go and trust will move you into the harmonic forces of pure, unconflicted desire—and out of the resistant vibrations of longing and discontent. In my own life, I can trace many wonderful events back to an original intention, but it was only when I moved from longing to surrender—and from need to present appreciation—that those dreams became reality.

5. Lack of Appreciation

The final negative energy that comes from an excessive focus on results is a lack of gratitude for what you already have. While it's perfectly natural to want a better life and to work on your goals, it *must* be done within the framework of present appreciation. If you can't (or won't) value your current life, it will be very difficult to draw more value to you.

You always have the option to choose your viewpoint. You're free to see the treasures around you and think, *I'm happy with what I have. I can find joy in my life right now.* Or you can concentrate on what's missing and think, *I need something else to be happy. Until it happens, I know I'll be miserable.*

But if you tend to live in the energy of the second worldview, be aware. Your attachment to the outcome is so extreme that your energy will actually push it away. This phenomenon of self-sabotage is called *paradoxical intent,* which we'll be exploring more thoroughly in the next chapter. For the moment, remember to make gratitude a strong intention right now.

When you attach your happiness—or anything else—to a future event, it defines your present experience as incomplete. This can't help but create a pervasive sense of lack! Your life-force vibration and your holistic consciousness are based in a positive view of yourself and your situation right now. To deny the value of the here-and-now is to dismiss the truth of your worthiness, as well as your power to create joy and positive perception. Gratitude is the consciousness shift that's required here.

Soulution

Present appreciation is a much stronger intention than future focus. Let yourself think about what you want, but really focus on being grateful for what you have. Recognize, acknowledge, and feel the wonder and value of all the blessings that exist within you and within your life. Spend some time every day in thanksgiving. No matter what may be going on, choose to find something to appreciate.

Your life is a work in progress, and every earthly experience can be valuable to you. It's time to stop making external, future events more important than achieving peace in your present process and recognizing the truth of your worth right now.

This very breath is a blessing; and as silly as it may seem, so is everything else, including the seat you're sitting on, the view in front of you, the clothes on your back, and this perfect instant in time. Stop right now and close your eyes. Hold this moment in your heart, and let yourself breathe in a deep appreciation for it. The fortune you seek is in this choice.

CHAPTER FOUR

THE CURSE OF LONGING

"I know that man cannot live by his own will alone. With his soul, he must search for the sources of the power of life. It is life we want."

— D. H. LAWRENCE

A deeper look at the function of intention is necessary for a complete approach to attraction. It's an important part of a complex and multilayered process that may not be as direct as you think. Layer upon layer of purposeful action, combined with life-force projection and personal perception, all go into the mix that creates the recipe for success.

But among the many misconceptions surrounding attraction is the simplicity with which these principles are viewed. While the core ideas are elegant in form and concept, if you study quantum physics, you'll find there are many diverse theories concerning consciousness and energy in the physical world. It follows that the human application of such ideas is also diverse. Just as there are countless paradoxes, dualities, and mysteries where energy and matter are concerned, there are many twists and turns in the multiple laws at work in the human experience.

LIE OF ATTRACTION

There is only one law and one formula for personal attraction: ask, believe, receive.

THE *REAL* TRUTH

Consciousness creation is a holistic—not simplistic—approach. There are many laws and many pieces in the puzzle of attraction. Belief is key; yet so are action, interaction, intention, harmony, presence, spirit, expansion, and surrender.

It's far too simplistic to whittle down the multifaceted principles of destiny creation to just one formula. Yet countless people sum up their approach to attraction in just three words: *ask, believe, receive.* While this is very good at its core, in many cases it only goes so far, revealing yet another half-truth that can actually lead to more frustration.

I'm not saying that this bare-bones approach doesn't work—I've used it successfully many times. Sometimes a thing that you want is so deeply ingrained in your destiny and consciousness that these three simple steps are all it takes to do the trick. Yet there are other times when your path of personal evolution is so complex that it takes a far greater depth of awareness and a much more layered approach just to move in the direction you desire.

Time, Tide, and Intention

People often look at end results and think that the process is linear, a step-by-step series of actions that clearly and predictably lead to the outcome. Sometimes that's the case. Yet as I look at my life and see the intentions that have come true—and those that have not—I realize that things have been more circuitous for me. The tide of my life has flowed in many different directions, and the detours I've taken along the way have been numerous. Such things as relationships, divorces, career changes, moves, sickness, school, children, and many other endeavors have provided me with much distraction—as well as joy and valuable information. Significant losses have brought lots of learning; and through it all, my goals and my life itself have been affected by my efforts and priorities.

When I was about 12 years old, I read a book that moved me so much that I decided that in addition to my plan to teach, I wanted to be a writer someday. It was the first time that mere words touched my heart, and I hoped that one day *my* words would be able to have a similar effect. I went to college to become a teacher, worked on my degree in secondary education, and planned to teach high school. Those thoughts about writing had moved to the recesses of my mind until around the time I was finishing my degree. At that point, I was again reading a very compelling book, only this one was on the *New York Times* bestseller list. One evening right before graduation, I was walking through the campus with some friends, and we all saw a shooting star. Somebody said, "Quick, make a wish," and everyone did so.

I don't know what my friends wished for, but I thought about the book I was reading and about the decision I'd made back in the seventh grade to someday become a writer. I figured if I was going to wish, I might as well wish big. I looked at that star and said to myself, *I want to be a writer—a New York Times best-selling writer.* I was 21 years old at the time, and I didn't really understand exactly what that wish meant—or how very long it would take before it happened.

I did become a teacher, though; and I started writing, too. It took 35 years and many, many (trust me—*many*) rejections and setbacks before the intention I made in that wish upon a star came true. In fact, it took about 15 years of writing just to get up the courage to self-publish my own work—then another 15 years to find my wonderful publisher, Hay House. When life (not intention) moved me from teaching to counseling, my writing took on an entirely different form, and my interest shifted completely. A lucky coincidence (was it really?) introduced me to quantum physics and charted my path for decades to come.

My career has been a long and winding road, but it's not the only place where I learned about life's idiosyncrasies and about the ins and outs of attraction and manifestation. The process I went through during my second divorce was very different from the first. By that time, I'd learned the principles of consciousness-created reality, and I finally realized I could take action to create something different. I knew I wanted to shift my own life force and send healthier expectations out into the Universe. Although I had some serious doubts about men, each night I projected my intention for love in a holographic visualization. I also made sure to support that by creating within myself the very same qualities that I wanted to attract in my partner. Amazingly, it only took a few short months before I met my husband. In that case, the line that connected intention, action, and result was clear.

Destiny's Detour

The same can't be said about my pursuit of a family. When I met my current husband, we decided to try to have children right away, but we were immediately and continually disappointed. I'd been teaching the principles of attraction and manifestation for many years by that time, so I pulled out all the stops. I did meditations, visualizations, and affirmations; and my husband and I prayed together each night. We both took herbs and followed nutritional and lifestyle advice that was designed to increase fertility. Short of in vitro fertilization, we did just about everything we could in order to get pregnant.

Yet that result was not to be a part of our destiny. The grief and sense of loss seemed to increase every month, and I had the same old reaction: *What am I doing (or thinking) wrong? Why can't I make this happen?* Each month, I visualized myself excitedly telling my family and friends that I was pregnant, and each month the sorrow struck anew. It felt like some big cosmic joke with the Universe saying, *You teach this stuff—if you really believed it, you should be able to do this.*

After enduring nearly two years of striving and self-torment, I finally gave up on that goal. In fact, it was the constant exertion that caused me to give up—not because it was so much effort, but because it just didn't seem natural anymore. It didn't resonate! For that reason, I felt it was time to move on. As much as it grieved me to do so, I started working on letting go of my dream of having children.

Not long after that, I met an attorney who dealt with foreign adoptions. I'd looked into adoption earlier, but I was told that I was too old to receive a child from domestic agencies. The same wasn't true in the world of foreign adoptions, however, so I started the long, arduous process of identifying and bringing home a child.

Believe it or not, this took eight years. Since my husband and I wanted to adopt children who were hard to place, we decided to look at the older kids that so few people ever consider. Because of the psychological and historical issues, it was a very important decision. To get the right match, we had to be especially particular about the agency. It took quite a while to find one that was willing to give us all the information we required, but it was worth the wait. We ended up bringing home two wonderful children: an 11-year-old boy and a 12-year-old girl. It's been more than ten years, and we know we were destined to be together. We all feel so blessed to have each other!

I now know why I wasn't granted my wish to get pregnant—and I also know why the striving had taken me so much out of balance with my own resonance. I was fighting my destiny—and the destiny of my adopted son and daughter! But even if that destiny had meant that I had no children at all, I needed to become willing to move in that direction and open up to other options that resonated with my heart and soul.

These experiences, along with many others, have taught me so much about the wonderful process that we call life—the being and becoming, the achieving and letting go. Through the ebb and flow, the happiness and hardships, I have to say that I've been blessed by it all. One of the biggest gifts I've received has been learning to live in paradox—and to be comfortable with uncertainty. It's an approach that brings such equanimity and peace. Energy is predictable, yet it can be very random. There are patterns in the chaos, and our real power lies not in forcing outcomes, but in understanding.

Okay with the Chaos

Whatever you're working toward, it's important to relax in the randomness and be calm in uncertainty. This is a far more magnetic energy than fussing and fretting over forcing your will. Become comfortable with contradictions, because there are plenty of them in these Truths about the Universal Laws:

- *Sometimes you know exactly what you want, and over time you can make it happen.*

- *Sometimes the Universe gives you a wonderful option that you never thought of before.*

- *Sometimes it takes a very long time to get what you're looking for, and there are many diversions along the way.*

- *Sometimes your goal happens immediately, and you find that it's just what you imagined.*

- *Sometimes when you achieve your goal, you find out that the experience isn't even close to what you had in mind.*

- *Sometimes you don't get what you want at all. It may be painful, but what you do get—whether in the form of a lesson or an entirely different result—can turn out to be far more valuable.*

These and other variables are true. But if you can't always predict the results, why use the laws at all? These principles aren't just about outcomes; they bring you strength in your understanding and in your process. They give you the power to change the present quality of your life, the very essence of your ongoing experience.

Soulution

The power of your consciousness and your vital energy definitely influence what you attract, but the results may turn up at some later point and in many unexpected and divergent ways. It all becomes easier when you look at your life as a process, and each experience as a precious stepping-stone.

Solutions come from moving forward, remaining open, and releasing control. Every day is an adventure, and every goal is an experiment. There are many paths to happiness. In fact, you can go there now.

So why intend—or work toward—anything? Even if there *is* some predictability, if there are other variables as well, why take the chance? The answer can be found in purpose and desire. That's the reason we're here and the reason we go on.

Whatever you're looking for, your genuine desire has a message for you. What it's telling you (and why) could be one of the most important perspectives in your life. It could mean a great deal of difference to you—and even to the world—to listen to your heart and find out what your longing has to say.

Why Desire?

Some Eastern philosophies teach that human desire is the source of all unhappiness. They say that if you can release your longings and let go of attachments, you'll not only achieve real happiness, you'll also reach enlightenment.

I find this philosophy fascinating, and when I can arrive at moments where all my longings and attachments are released, I can feel that peace—and profoundly sense the wisdom in that choice. With the right kind of attitude, real happiness can indeed come from an unencumbered and unattached life.

But does this necessarily make every desire bad? I can't believe that's the case. Wanting things can be motivating and inspiring. It has driven the human race forward in wonderful and even miraculous ways. Desire has created great art, scientific and technological discoveries, and entire movements of humanitarianism and spiritual growth.

But what about your personal goals? As an individual, you're probably less likely to seek enlightenment through detachment than you are to seek achievement through your dreams and desires. The big question is: how far can you let yourself go into the desire zone without becoming too invested and attached?

⚖

Lie of Attraction

The deeper your desire—and the more emotional the intention—the more likely it will come true, and the faster that will happen.

The *Real* Truth

The emotions of enthusiasm and excitement are excellent energy conductors. But if your desire becomes desperate or urgent, then you're actually overly attached, creating the sabotaging energies of *paradoxical intent.*

As with so many issues of attraction, the energy of your desire will shift according to the meaning you attach to it. As soon as you make something mean too much—or give it too much value or power in your life—it becomes an obsession. The fact is, you simply can't be fixated on anything whether it's a goal, a person, a substance, a place, or anything else—without eventually becoming miserable. The constant thinking and striving around your obsession takes up too much energy to allow you to maintain a life of real peace and authentic power. And when anything destroys your present peace, it shifts the value and meaning not only of the thing itself, but also of your life and even your self-perception!

This is where you can get into trouble—when not having your desire has the power to make you miserable. It's a normal part of the human experience to long for things like love, wisdom, creative expression, and personal and career achievement. All of these pursuits are healthy and can promote an inner sense of joy and peace. The problem comes when you lose your joy and peace because your desire has consumed you. When the longing becomes desperate, fearful, or urgent, your life force becomes miserable; and your desire becomes unhealthy and far less likely to be supported in the energetic realm.

This is one of the reasons why some people feel so frustrated—even to the point of hopelessness—about their dreams. They dutifully visualize what they want, affirm it every day, and contemplate its presence in their life. They think they've dedicated themselves to their goal, but they don't realize that their feelings have switched from dedication to desperation, and from mere desire to urgent need. As a result, instead of attraction, many individuals are experiencing increasing frustration and deeper longing. They've unwittingly moved into the toxic energies of paradoxical intent; and the more they ask, the more distant the solution seems to get.

Paradoxical Intent: Desire's Dead End

Some goals are driven by personal purpose, such as the search for meaning, wisdom, discovery, or expression. Even if an intention seems more worldly—such as finding love or becoming an entrepreneur—if your desire is balanced and honoring to yourself and others, then its energy is pure. This heartfelt resonance has a much greater likelihood of success in the energetic realm and in the real world. Although there are many variables, and the outcome may not take shape in exactly the time and way you imagined, the odds of achievement are much greater with the energies of trust and surrender.

If, on the other hand, your desire is driven by urgency, ego, or fear, the odds of getting what you want will drop dramatically. Of course, you may be able to find the love or create the business, but what you experience in those perceived achievements may not resemble what you were looking for at all. The bottom line is that you can either propel or poison your desire by the meaning you attach to it.

> *The* ***Law of Paradoxical Intent*** *says that the more desperate you are to make something happen, the more your needy energy will push the goal away and create the opposite—or the paradox—of your intent. However, the more you let go and perceive your desire as just another way to enhance an already-happy life, the more you'll draw joyful results to you.*

We've all experienced this phenomenon at least once. We long for something so desperately that it becomes a guiding beacon for all of our attention, emotion, and time. We become convinced that such a profoundly deep desire has to be met. Unfortunately, we don't realize that we may be putting roadblocks in our own way, creating obstacles of toxic attachment.

The Law of Paradoxical Intent is a powerful force and dynamic influence on our earthly experience. Most people are completely unaware when they've slipped into this negative energy, but it's important to become conscious of this vital piece of the attraction and manifestation puzzle.

To get clarity, you need to ask yourself: *What am I making the achievement of this goal mean?* Your awareness of your motivation can change everything. If you need something to be happy, you can guarantee present unhappiness. If you believe that your goal will bring completion or security, you're destined to feel incomplete and insecure. The paradox is, the more you seek something out of desperation, the more your life force of need and anxiety will stop it cold.

Red Flags of Desperation

I've seen the effects of paradoxical intent countless times in my life and in the lives of my clients. When you're needy and urgent about something, you push it away; but when you let the attachment go, it (or something even better) will come your way. It may seem like some cosmic joke, but this reversal of outcome isn't the only reason to release the self-sabotaging pattern of excessive need.

Desperation is poison to your goals, but far more important is its effect on your life. Your assignment of extraordinary meaning to your goal can agitate you on a constant basis, creating a current of unhappiness that runs deeply through your daily experience. This river of misery picks you up and takes you to unintended and unknown energetic and emotional places. The more deeply you invest, the more the unhappiness current picks up speed and becomes the major direction of your life.

Soulution

The power of your consciousness can help release your desperation. Left unchecked, your need and frustration will become an ongoing problem—not just a temporary disruption that you can cycle through. But by changing the meaning you assign to your goals, you can shift your entire life experience—and your results as well.

Take a moment to answer these questions:

- *What has your goal come to mean to you?*
- *Do your thoughts about it make you feel peaceful and enthusiastic or urgent and needy?*
- *Which emotion is more likely to bring success?*

Remember, it's the attachment and meaning you give to your goals that will either help or hinder the process. The following beliefs are important signs that you're getting into the dangerous seas of paradoxical intent. Identify your own red flags, and use the *Soul*-ution response after each item to navigate into calmer waters. If you make genuine and consistent intentions, you'll soon find that things will be smooth sailing.

⚖

Desperate Belief #1:
I need this to be happy.

This is the most common self-sabotaging energy that you could fall into. The problem is, this belief plainly tells the Universe (and you) that you're incapable of being happy now. Your energetic message is clear: *Don't bother sending me anything; I won't be able to enjoy it anyway.*

Not only does this conclusion destroy the quality of your daily life, but your choice to give up present peace and joy while longing for a future unknown creates a miserable life force. This will not only generate resistance against your desire, it will block other good things as well.

> ***Soulution:*** *I create my own happiness every day. I choose to find joy in myself and my life right now, and I attract more joy to me.*

Happiness isn't merely a fleeting experience that comes and goes according to the outer events of your life. It's a pervasive attitude, a state of being that you can choose to live in regardless of externals. It's your responsibility to reawaken yourself to the potential for joy in every moment. Recognize every opportunity for bliss, and be grateful for it.

Create the intention to make genuine happiness—not just pleasure—one of the primary qualities of your life. Don't wait for it! Do it; choose it; live it now.

Desperate Belief #2:
I would feel so much better about myself if I could make this happen.

Many people seek their self-approval through some kind of achievement. Whether it's being in a relationship, getting a degree or a promotion, or just losing weight, they believe the accomplishment itself will finally allow them to accept themselves.

This is a truly dangerous precedent to set! No matter what you achieve, you'll continue to pin your self-esteem on things and people outside of you. The striving and seeking will never end until you *choose* to approve of yourself once and for all.

Soulution: *I deserve to accept myself just as I am. I choose to love and value myself without condition now.*

Becoming the source of your self-approval is absolutely necessary for both happiness and a magnetic life force. You deserve your own high regard, so you need to affirm the truth of your worthiness, value, and power every single day.

The consciousness of genuine self-love is perhaps the most important one that you can establish. Affirm it and meditate on it. Make it a heartfelt approach in your view and treatment of yourself—and in your approach to all your goals.

Desperate Belief #3:
This will show other people how really wonderful I am.

You may not realize it, but you may be looking at your goal as a way to express your worth, intellect, beauty, or talent to others. This is closely connected to the element of self-approval, but it actually creates even more striving and desperation. It may be natural to want to express yourself, to demonstrate your talent and intellect, but when you need some external achievement to know these things are true, you poison the energy and intention around your goal.

Whenever you require anything outside of you to show the world (or yourself) how valuable you are, you're attaching way too much meaning to it. Work on the goal for its own sake, not as evidence of your worth. You'll be amazed by what a difference it makes.

Soulution: *I am valuable and worthy just as I am. When I bring honor and love to myself and the world, all that I do is worthwhile.*

Nothing outside of you increases your intrinsic value. It's inherent to yourself, sourced in your Divine legacy and your soul's eternal identity. What you choose to do may be important to the world, but if you do it just to raise yourself up, its energy will be tainted.

Intend honor—not glory—and that will bring more of both vibrations to you and to all of us.

Desperate Belief #4:
My life is incomplete without this.

When you use an achievement to define you or complete your life, you're walking a very thin line. What happens when that goal isn't met? Or if it is achieved, what happens if it goes away?

Your choice to define yourself by anything external depletes your power and shifts your energy into need and negativity. After all, thinking your life is incomplete makes it impossible to truly appreciate what you have, and you just can't attract without present appreciation.

Soulution: *Only I define myself. I live a full and complete life every single day.*

As with self-acceptance and valuing, you absolutely must choose to define yourself separately, internally, and eternally. A goal does *not* define you—nor does a job or another person. Your definition preceded these things and will extend beyond them. If you persist in this assumption, you'll only be disappointed, for everything—*everything*—on this earthly plane is transitory.

So seek a deeper meaning; find value and completion from a higher source. Look into your eternal heart and soul, and remember who you are!

Desperate Belief #5:
This is my only option . . . if this doesn't happen, I'm doomed.

You may get so desperate that you arrive at an all-or-nothing view of what you want to achieve. This extends need and urgency into accelerated measures. When you believe there's only one solution, you become so frantic, and your life force becomes so agitated, that the fearful energy will stop the accomplishment cold. Not only that, it limits your options, receptivity, flexibility, and creativity. As a result, this attitude is downright disastrous to both your happiness and the achievement of your goal.

***Soul*ution:** *I have plenty of options.*
I am flexible and willing to see
the many choices open to me.
I even have the ability to be happy now.

There's never only one person, one job, or one solution to a problem. Your life could take many paths, and you never know what awaits you on the road ahead.

Open yourself to the guidance of spirit and the abundance of the Universe. Always remember that your options for unattached happiness exist already.

⚖

Surrender is a key ingredient in the process of attraction. It's also a remarkable tool for life itself. It doesn't mean giving up; it just means detaching, letting go of overinvestment and the need for control. These are the things that really make you unhappy, so why hold on to them?

When you invest the emotional quality of your life in specific external outcomes, you put yourself at the mercy of the outer world. *Yet one of the greatest goals in life is equanimity—establishing inner peace without any dependence on external factors.* The paradox is this: a tranquil, unattached approach creates such a gentle and beautiful vibration in the world that the externals you seek invariably start to flow your way. And if you do hit a cycle that may have some challenges, you always have the inner clarity and wisdom to respond with strength and soul-centered resilience.

You may be immersed in the workings of the world, but remember: your spirit provides the solutions. Make its light, love, and eternal strength the goals you long for most. Your soul is the one thing you can invest in with certainty, the driving truth you can freely attach to without hesitation. In fact, in all the mysteries of life, it's your eternal soul that can bring the most power and resolution.

So take a moment to let everything go and feel the peace that simple surrender can bring. Let go of the fear and be still. Your spirit is whispering deep within. Listen closely, and know that it has answers for you.

PART II

MYSTERIES of CREATION

"From science and from the spiritual experience of millions, we are discovering our capacity for endless awakenings in a universe of endless surprises."

— MARILYN FERGUSON

CHAPTER FIVE

LIFE, LAWS, AND TOGETHERNESS

"This, I thought, is how great visionaries and poets see everything—as if for the first time. Each morning they see a new world before their eyes; they do not really see it, they create it."

— NIKOS KAZANTZAKIS

At this point, you may be wondering what the whole story of attraction is. Well, to discover that, it's helpful to step back and look at the big picture. As you've seen, the process of attraction is more complex than most people think, and things aren't always as they seem.

Standing on planet Earth, it looks flat, and the colors around you vary with the location and season. But from outer space, Earth looks spherical; and since the predominant element is water, its color is blue. Here, you may be looking at the colorless ground and gray sky of winter;

but from a distance, your home is a beautiful blue ball with white clouds drifting around it.

Your energy is like that—a different experience when you're standing in the middle of it than when you step back and look at the big picture. There are so many things that need to be considered, both inside and out. The entire image gives a clearer view and a far greater understanding of where you are and what your energy really says about you.

So if you were your own little planet, what would you look like from a distance? Would your energy be small and red like Mars? Would your presence be large like Jupiter, or perhaps surrounded by the influence of those around you, such as the rings of Saturn? Step out of your immediate issues for a moment and take a look at the big picture where your entire life is concerned.

Manifesting a Life (Rather Than Things or Events)

The process that we call life is truly mysterious. There are some certainties, such as the fact that day will follow night, and many likelihoods, such as the potential for rain in the spring. Yet there are countless variables that can't be predicted, and it's there that we seem to get lost.

People are afraid of the unknown—that's why they stay in situations they hate. This choice gives them a false sense of knowing, and they think, *If I just stay put, I can predict what will happen.* Instead of embracing doubt or seeing the adventure in the unknown, their drive for certainty and false control makes them willing to give away their real power and personal control.

It's tempting to think that you can determine the future and direct all the events of your life according to will. In fact, there's a lot of truth in your ability to plan and intend the results that you desire. But it's important to see the big picture, consider all the factors, and realize that there are many things that may still be unknown. When you employ your personal powers yet remain open to the unknown variables, you walk the middle ground of directing and observing, allowing and learning.

It's actually quite liberating to define your goals not as the main event, but as just one part of the bigger picture. It frees you from obsessive anxiety when you view the process rather than the problems. It also empowers and enlightens you when you focus on the whole of your existence rather than limiting your thoughts to what you want to have happen in the near future.

The truth is, if you wish to utilize the laws of attraction to the best of your ability, this holistic approach is the way to go. All of life is energy, and your vibration is a palpable and influential presence in the world. To access the entirety of your energy, you need to consider every aspect of your life. If you pour all of your attention into just one goal, you not only miss wonderful opportunities and present experiences, you also miss important lessons that can bring about profound clarity, growth, and even the joy that may be waiting elsewhere.

Don't marginalize your own life! It's crazy to put yourself on the sidelines while you're frantically striving to make things better!

Each day, you're weaving the tapestry of your earthly experience, so it's far more productive to make your *entire life* your intention. Every part of your experience is worth the effort; and when you come from a grander point of view, all of the factors will seem to fall into place more easily. From this open and interested perspective, you'll become aware of things you never even thought of—and you'll be empowered by the laws of attraction and all the other elements of creation.

The Five Factors of Destiny Creation

Just as there are many theories, laws, and phenomena in quantum physics, there are also many influences on the human experience. When you study natural and physical events, you'll find terms such as *weak and strong force, uncertainty, chaos,* and *complexity,* to name just a few of the many astounding principles of the physical world.

There's still a lot to learn about these aspects of the Universe. And there's just as much—perhaps even more—to discover about the workings of human energy in this process we call life. We can at least investigate what we do know, however, and see how the various pieces of the attraction puzzle fit together.

There are five main influences on our destiny creation:

1. The Laws of Attraction
2. The Soul's Intention and Spirit Cycles
3. The Cycles of Life
4. Karmic Cycles
5. Shared Consciousness

All of these play a part in how, when, and why we get the results we do. We're going to be exploring each item in detail, but first let's get an overview of what these attraction factors are.

Factor 1: The Laws of Attraction

Although there are many laws, they work together because they're all based on your personal powers of consciousness, energy, and intention. Each law responds to a specific cause and effect in your life, which I'll be talking about later in this chapter. The important thing to remember, however, is that the laws represent patterns of potentiality—powerful forces that you can tap into in order to help you move forward. While the laws aren't the only element of destiny creation, keeping them in mind and understanding their purpose will significantly assist you in successfully dealing with anything and everything that life may send your way.

Factor 2: The Soul's Intention and Spirit Cycles

You can deny it if you want, but you do have an eternal identity; and your soul has its own intentions. Unfortunately, they may be entirely different from your personal intentions of making money or achieving success. In spite of this split, your spirit can be a driving force in your experiences. If you dismiss this, you'll be ignoring a huge piece of the attraction puzzle. You may be wondering why something is happening to you, and you can investigate your energy and thoughts, but you may have to go even further than that. In fact, your spirit may hold the key to what has happened and what will be. The truth is that when you align your soul's intention with your goals, you'll unlock all the mysteries and open the door to ultimate abundance.

Factor 3: The Cycles of Life

In terms of spirit, we do have unlimited power, and I believe that there will come a time when we can transcend the parameters of earthly life by virtue of our thinking alone. Someday we all may be able to fly in the air, walk on water, and never die. But at this point in time, we've contracted to live according to the general requirements of this physical experience—that means birth, death, age, and sometimes illness. These are just some of the cycles of life that our destiny carries. Even within these experiences, we're capable of great miracles. We just need to know how to bring our consciousness to each cycle in order to deal with and heal what's real.

Factor 4: Karmic Cycles

Your energy may change, but it will *not* end. As you move from life to life, your eternal consciousness becomes encoded and carries information with it. That encrypted data, along with the vibrational memories of the past, may be having a vast influence on what you're attracting today. But old traumas and difficulties can be cleared and released, yielding more power in the present to activate a brighter future.

Factor 5: Shared Consciousness

As human beings, we make all sorts of connections. We link with our family members, co-workers, communities, and even other groups we may not be aware of. The energy we all share can have an effect on our personal path. This is the power of shared consciousness, a vortex of momentum that gathers strength and expands beyond our knowing. In this and the following chapters, we'll take a look at the element of shared consciousness, find out how it impacts our lives, and learn how to deal with it in productive and beneficial ways. Yes, we all influence each other—and together, we direct the destiny of the world.

⚖

All of these are important influences in the ongoing experiences of our lives. Understanding their presence is vital to our process and happiness for three reasons. First, it allows us to get out of our egos and investigate the higher meaning of things. Second, this objective overview then helps us release self-blame and become more proactive. Finally, understanding these influences makes it easier to shift our thoughts and our consciousness because we have the information we need.

When we run into some roadblocks, we don't have to panic. Instead, we can stop and look at the big picture in order to view all the elements at play. Rather than faulting ourselves, we can take our power back and then apply all of the laws to the situations we're in. When we see things with clarity and apply healthy interpretations and self-actualized plans to any circumstance, we can finally break free from outer obstacles, as well as our own inner patterns of resistance. With this self-aware approach, we can take the steps needed to move forward to a far better life.

Law Practice

There are at least seven laws of attraction that represent the patterns of energy and consciousness in the human experience. They can be very powerful tools when applied to your choices in belief, behavior, and lifestyle.

Don't take the "law" metaphor too literally, though. These aren't legal requirements that will punish you if you disobey. They're more like the natural laws that point out some predictability in the physical world. Similar to the law of gravity, they're impartial—not punitive. If you were to drop an egg on the floor, the law of gravity wouldn't be punishing you by causing it to break. No, the egg would break merely as a natural response to that law being in play in your universe.

The laws of attraction are the same way—there's no punishment there. What happens is merely a function of your energy and consciousness moving out in the world, responding to the laws and other influential factors in order to contribute to the formation of your life experiences.

This is why understanding the nature of all the laws is so important. Your personal powers of consciousness, energy, and intent are very real forces in the world. Instead of living an unconscious life and reacting without awareness, it's possible to wake up and realize that you can change your responses. You can gently shift your thoughts and beliefs without obsession or self-blame.

When you take a sane and active approach to all of these principles, you can transform the nature of your life.

1. The Law of Manifestation

This first law of attraction is based on a fundamental, very active force in both the world and your life. Modern physicists accept the theory of *consciousness-created reality,* which can be applied to everything from cosmological beginnings to the individual experiences of the human being.

> *The* ***Law of Manifestation*** *says that your consciousness creates your reality. This is projected in your self-view, worldview, and expectations, which send a holographic image of yourself and your life force out into the world. This holistic understanding is very powerful. Even a small shift in consciousness can create a dramatic change in results.*
>
> ***Key components:*** *Positive self- and worldviews and a life force of vitality and optimism*

As discussed earlier, success doesn't merely refer to specific thoughts bringing about specific results. It's a matter of projecting a life force that's filled with positive images and conclusions of confidence, optimism, and self-love. Since your consciousness relies heavily on your view of yourself and your personal expectations, it will be very difficult to create success if you consistently engage in self-judgment, and pessimism about your future. But you can intentionally lift your awareness to a more positive perception of yourself, your environment, and the day ahead. This will transform your consciousness and help shift the reality you create.

Your greatest power for change can be found in your awareness. Even if you can't change the situation you're in, you can still shift how you perceive it. It's your interpretation of what's around you—and not the circumstances themselves—that will ultimately determine the quality of your experience and the power of your life force.

I've seen the law of consciousness-created reality at work many times in my life. One particular story involves Dr. Wayne W. Dyer, who's a wonderful author and inspiring motivational speaker.

About 20 years ago, I attended a conference where Wayne and a few other authors spoke. In his lecture, Wayne talked about a discussion that he and the other authors had over dinner the night before. I thought, *Someday I'd like to speak at a conference with Wayne and have dinner with him and the other authors.* I even took a moment to visualize it, but not having any idea how it would happen, I let it go.

I didn't think about it much after that, largely because my whole life force had become about something that was far more important to me—teaching genuine self-love and the principles of personal consciousness and energy. I was publishing my own book back then and even doing lectures for free. I was passionate about the information, and I really wanted to share it with others and help people make their lives better.

I did attend more of Wayne's lectures, and when I did, I would remember that old intention. There were times when I could feel it happening, and other times when it just didn't resonate. It didn't matter either way, however, because my entire life was now driven by a consciousness of personal purpose and enthusiasm.

My career hit many delays and roadblocks along the way, but I maintained an optimistic attitude, and I was so inspired by the process and the information, I was able to keep moving forward. About ten years after that original intention about Wayne had come to mind, my wonderful publisher, Hay House, picked up my first book. Shortly before that, Wayne had switched publishers and gone to Hay House, also.

In a few more years, I found myself speaking at the Hay House I Can Do It!® conference along with Wayne and many other fantastic people. At the authors' dinner on one Saturday night, I told him about my old intention.

I said, "A long time ago, I visualized us speaking together and having dinner . . ."

He jumped up, gave me a hug, and ended my sentence by saying, ". . . and here we are."

This is just one of the many fun experiences that have come my way. But it goes to show how your entire consciousness creates your reality. One fleeting intention—backed by a purpose-driven life force—can make something happen.

So formulate your own consciousness based on positive self-perception and a purposeful and optimistic worldview. Gently let go of any pessimistic thoughts, and remember that you get to decide what is true for you. Prioritize your *whole life* over any individual outcome; and fill your days with passion, enthusiasm, and self-love.

2. The Law of Magnetism

Unlike the first law, which is about creation or manifestation, this law is about attraction. As such, this is what most people consider to be the single law of attraction, and it's true that its principles are based on the exchange and return of energy—your energy.

> *The **Law of Magnetism** states that the Universe returns the same kind of energy that you put out about yourself. This last part is an important piece that many people miss. Your self-treatment, self-care, and self-talk are significant sources of your emotions and energetic resonance.*
>
> ***Key components:*** *Self-honoring, self-respect, and personal responsibility for genuine happiness*

More than anything else, the return on your energy will reflect two things: how you treat yourself and how much responsibility you take for your own present and authentic happiness. It will be difficult to receive good treatment and high priority from the Universe if you don't give that to yourself first—and equally hard to attract happy events if you're always miserable.

Clearing up energy requires more than randomly changing your thoughts, however. It's getting to the root of your unhappiness—changing the lies that you've been living and starting to dwell in truth. You're going to be exploring this more deeply in Part III, but until then, remember the issue of self-honoring. When this gets integrated into your signature resonance, you'll be amazed by how much better you feel about yourself, and you'll soon see much happier returns.

Your personal vibration is also made up of your emotional resonance. If you're unhappy all the time, it's up to you to change things. This is where a lot of people get sidetracked. They confuse mere pleasure with genuine happiness, and they end up derailing themselves completely.

When you read about the law of attraction, you're often told that you only attract good things by feeling good now. I know this advice is well intended, encouraging you to shift from unhappiness to joy in order to change your emotional resonance; but somehow important elements have gotten lost in translation.

Of course, it's critical to create a positive and blissful emotional resonance, but that's not done through merely feeling good or denying what makes you unhappy. It's done through resolving it. Genuine happiness isn't a Band-Aid approach. You have to explore the source of the problem and deal with it in ways that are honoring to both yourself and others. Escapism, denial, and even mindless affirmations just won't do. You must get to the core of what's wrong and take responsibility for healing it.

I recently heard an amazing story of how the admonition to feel good went terribly awry. After reading something on the law of attraction, a man in his 40s decided he wasn't happy and didn't want to project those negative vibes anymore. So in order to feel good, he took his savings, abandoned his wife and two small children, and went to the tropics with a young woman he'd recently met. He did all this because he wasn't feeling good, but he was never really willing to find out why. He may be happier at the moment, but his energy contradicted so many of the laws, I can pretty much guarantee it won't last long.

Genuine happiness is a lifestyle attitude. It's a willingness to see value, appreciate blessings, and work out problems in appropriate and honoring ways. Of course, if you're in a situation that doesn't honor you, you'll need to deal with that—and you may even need to leave it, but do so by following healthy and appropriate steps. Start with investigating ways you can bring more honoring choices to yourself and your life. Get up every day with the intention to be responsible for your own genuine happiness. Both of these actions create wonderful vibrations that are attractive to others and to the Universe itself.

3. The Law of Pure Desire

While the other laws reflect your consciousness and energy, the Law of Pure Desire is the first of two laws that respond to your intentions.

> *The **Law of Pure Desire** says that beneficial outcomes are generated by pure and clear intentions. They're not based in fear or manipulation. A goal framed in pure desire is healthy, flexible, and designed to enhance—not complete—your life.*
>
> ***Key components:** Genuine motivation, trust, and unconflicted intentions*

When you pursue your goals out of fear, you bog them down in toxic energy that could easily sabotage your results. But if your motivations are genuine—if the goal is healthy and intended to enhance an already-happy life of your own making—then the vibration surrounding your desire is pure and magnetic.

To maintain clarity of desire, it's also important to be aware if you're having any thoughts that lead you in opposite directions. You may say you want a husband, but also think that there are no good men to be found. You may intend to look for a job, all the while telling yourself that nobody's hiring.

These are *conflicting intentions*. They generate fear, split your motivation, and fragment your energy. In cases of such opposing intents, the Universe will simply not know which one to serve. Does it go with the desire to find a good man, or does it respond to the belief that he doesn't exist? Your mixed message will cancel itself out.

But pure desire is based in trust with clear, unconflicted intentions. When you bring these energies to your pursuits, the results are much more likely to be beneficial—and even more accelerated.

A friend of mine recently saw the power of this law in her life. Jeannie had always had job issues. Either positions were hard to find, they weren't to her liking, or they ended too soon. As a result, she'd always acted desperate and panic stricken whenever she found herself out of work.

This dilemma surfaced for her again last year. Her entire department was cut, and she had to find another job. This time, however, she did things differently. Instead of panicking, she was methodical and trusting. She put out résumés in numerous places and contacted former co-workers to check on openings in her field.

Within a few months, Jeannie got a job she loved. Not only that, within the year, she purchased her very first home. In the past, she'd always refused to buy a house because she'd been afraid that she couldn't handle the responsibility or even be sure of making the payments. But now she continued the reversal of her fearful energy, reinforcing the new trust she had in herself and in her intentions.

Like Jeannie, you can reverse old patterns of doubt and fear, and implement the key components of pure desire. By releasing conflicting intentions and engaging in trust and genuine motivation, you can accelerate your own results. You'll also be able to avoid the negative patterns of the next law.

4. The Law of Paradoxical Intent

This law also deals with your motives, requiring them to be free of desperation and urgency. Although much of Chapters 3 and 4 investigated the perilous energies of this law, let's recap it here.

> *The **Law of Paradoxical Intent** says that the more desperate you are to achieve a certain goal, the more your urgent, needy energy will sabotage the results and push it away.*
>
> ***Key components:** Surrendering attachment and letting go of urgency by engaging in a self-actualized and peaceful pursuit*

Most of us have experienced a point in our lives where we were desperate to achieve something. We felt we needed that particular person or thing in order to make us happy. Unfortunately, this urgent need can make us so miserable that it totally distorts our magnetic energy. It creates agitation, unhappiness, and even hopelessness—definitely not the energies that can bring us joy or positive results. In short, desperation is poison to desire.

The solution comes from pursuing your goals without assuming that your happiness is attached to them. As you've seen with the other laws, genuine happiness is an important core vibration in your life force. So if you're putting that on hold while waiting for some future event, your lack of present joy will make it impossible to achieve a blissful outcome in the future.

But you can switch your approach and transform the results. Let go of desperation and change it to determination instead. Engage in a peaceful and persistent pursuit of your goal, with a willingness to enjoy the process for however long it takes. You may need to be flexible and readjust your plan, but when you make self-established happiness your present attitude, you'll become more creative, more productive, and much more able to see things through.

Such was the case for a client of mine named Miranda, who was attempting to get pregnant. She and her husband had become so desperate that she was living in constant anxiety and frustration. After nearly two years of trying with no results, they decided it was time to let that need go. They wanted to relax, so they took a short vacation where they did some sightseeing, got massages, and had a perfectly enjoyable and relaxed time. They were at peace with their decision to let go—but that wasn't the end of the story.

About a month after returning from their vacation, Miranda found out that she was pregnant. She and her husband had released their desperation to conceive and had opened their lives to finding joy in other ways. Once Miranda was able to totally relax, she reversed her needy energy and got what she was looking for. She now has a beautiful baby boy, and she says that she never lets herself feel desperate about anything anymore.

As is often the case with the energies of paradoxical intent, when you let go of the attachment and surrender the needs, a beneficial result shows up in your life. More important, when you engage in true surrender, you know that your happiness is sourced within—not based in anything external to you.

5. The Law of Harmony

This law reveals how you can align yourself with the synchronistic flow of the Universe. By creating a more harmonic vibration, you can move into the natural rhythm of abundance.

> *The **Law of Harmony** says that when you live in peace and balance, you move into alignment with Source energy. By consciously reducing the conflict in yourself and your life, you raise your vibration to a higher level of attraction and manifestation.*
>
> ***Key components:*** *Choices that promote personal balance and inner and outer peace, as well as a pervasive sense of equality and connection with all others*

The first form of harmony is with the self. Choose to let go of the conflict within your own mind. Bring a greater sense of balance to your everyday choices, and make present peace a real intention. By releasing worry, striving, and self-hostility, you can create a more harmonic personal resonance.

Harmony with others starts with the realization that we're all connected, equal in our value and worthiness to receive. This is an important truth that must be embraced if you want your life to vibrate with peace instead of conflict. Your acceptance of yourself and others puts you on equal footing. It authentically empowers you, and the connection brings you assistance from unexpected sources.

Finally, harmonize yourself with Divine consciousness and with all of the Universe. The kind of peace that this connection brings is unstoppable. When you acknowledge the presence of the Divine within yourself and everything around you, the feelings of love and tranquility are palpable. When in harmony, your energy vibrates with such eternal truth that it will unite your intentions with the power of creation itself.

6. The Law of Right Action

This law is most commonly called the Law of Cause and Effect. It's similar to the Law of Magnetism, but instead of the Universe returning energy that reflects your self-treatment, in this case, it returns what you project onto others.

> *The* ***Law of Right Action*** *says that the more you treat others with value, honor, dignity, and compassion, the more those beautiful energies will return to you.*
>
> ***Key components:*** *Respectful and compassionate behavior, loving intention, and integrity*

The Law of Right Action requires you to be kind to yourself and civil and caring to others. Your choices in this regard have a big impact on the quality of energy you carry with you. Self-honoring gives you a core of authentic strength, and being compassionate to others actually increases your power in the world. On the other hand, fearing others will make you feel powerless, while bringing judgment and hostility to them will reduce your own vibration of honor and dignity. When choosing right action, you have to remember that honoring goes both ways.

The benefits of this law are stimulated by integrity, compassion, and caring intention. Love is a constant and conscious choice. When freely extended, its incomparable energy moves both inward and outward. Caring for others doesn't mean you have to deny yourself; it actually expands your own experience of love.

Caring intentions are full of tenderness, forgiveness, and compassion. Whether directed to yourself or to friends and loved ones—or even universally to all humankind—every single intention of love weaves a heart-to-heart connection that moves you into the flow of the energy's creative force. This is a fluid and powerful current that runs through the world, creating results whenever it's engaged.

The love and reverence you bring to those around you will return many times over. Your choice to engage in compassion and right action will be greatly appreciated by the shared consciousness, and the blessings you receive will reflect that.

7. The Law of Expanding Influence

This law demonstrates how others' energy influences you and how yours reaches out to affect the people in your life, along with every other soul.

> *The **Law of Expanding Influence** reveals that your personal energy expands in the world. In addition to creating your own results, your attitude and actions move out to determine consequences in others' lives and in the world at large. Conversely, the energy of others has an impact on your own experiences. This is true for everyone, but especially for the people you connect with—your family members, friends, co-workers, and affiliated groups of all kinds.*
>
> ***Key components:** Peaceful shared and individual consciousness; increased awareness of energy patterns; and expansion, connection, and influence*

For real success, it's necessary to understand the finer nuances of all the laws, and this one is especially important. Your energy field is affected by those around you, and by virtue of a phenomenon known as *quantum interconnectedness,* you have the same impact on them. This means that the people in your sphere can help enhance or reduce the quality of the vibration you send out to the world. So you need to be conscious of (but not obsessed with) the energy of those whom you repeatedly interact with. Reduce your exposure to fearful or critical individuals, if you can. Set boundaries and express your desire to be more peaceful and optimistic.

Sometimes you may be forced through family ties or work situations to be among people whose attitudes may be somewhat toxic to you. Don't fret about it too much. Visualize yourself in a bubble of light, where the negative energy bounces off you and becomes neutralized. If things get too pessimistic, say, "I prefer not to talk about this," and let yourself walk away.

When you're removing yourself from an interaction like that, always visualize yourself leaving the negative energy behind. As you go out the door, bless everyone involved. Affirm that you're free from their influence and that you're choosing to create happy and uplifting energy in your life. Determine what honors you, and follow your intuition in those situations.

It's also important to know that your action expands as well. If you're working on a goal, do as much in as many different directions as you can. Don't be frantic about it, but investigate your options. If one way doesn't work, try another. The solution may not come in the manner you expect, but your expanding action tells the Universe that you're serious about your intention and that you're open to the various results it could provide.

Shared Consciousness and Destiny Creation

There's a much bigger element in the Law of Expanding Influence. The phenomenon of shared consciousness refers to more than just the impact of our friends and acquaintances. It's the effect we have on the world—and that its energy has on us. That's right! You and I can actually sway the shared destiny of the whole world!

This global influence is a function of what's called the *M-field,* an abbreviation for the term *Morphogenetic field,* coined by author Rupert Sheldrake in his book *A New Science of Life.* Basically, this is the phenomenon where we as individuals feed great consciousness fields of information and energy. Those fields then expand in the shared consciousness of all humankind.

Each of us contributes our own unique vibration to a group consciousness. The more of a certain type of energy is fed into the field, the more that momentum builds, expanding in a process called *morphic resonance.* When a critical magnitude is reached, that specific energy moves out and influences everyone on the planet.

Shared consciousness is easy to see in groups and movements. Information eras such as the Enlightenment, the Renaissance, the Industrial Revolution, and more recently, the digital age, have all grown in momentum and have changed the face and destiny of the world.

In fact, our world is changing even now. Have you noticed how time seems to have sped up? Everything is accelerating; from fast food to high-speed Internet, people are taking less time to do more things. I've talked to countless individuals of all ages, and virtually everyone has noticed this phenomenon. They feel as though they're on a treadmill—there are more tasks; and there is more effort, less time, and less leisure.

Perhaps it's a function of the Internet's expanding influence, but it seems as if we've been drawn into a collective unconscious of urgency. And as we feel time speeding up, we hurry through our lives and then feed that M-field ourselves, causing the acceleration to grow even further. It's ironic, because the need for speed in tasks and communication has actually increased individual isolation—another M-field energy that seems to be growing.

It seems as if we're all being swept up in this accelerated consciousness, but it's going to be very important to rein in the momentum of this particular morphic resonance. For the health and happiness of the individual, to reduce isolation and loneliness, and even for the health of the planet and the peace of the world itself, we must consciously slow things down.

We need to make leisure, balance, and face-to-face interaction more important. This may take conscious effort, however, because in this day and age, these things can be amazingly difficult to achieve. In days gone by, nature used to force a certain amount of peace and balance upon us. We had to stop working when the sun went down. Daylight, distance, and the seasons pretty much restricted our options to overdo things.

But technology and transportation have changed all that. Now we have the option to work all night—and we often do. We can fly from place to place, expect to be able to adjust to different time zones automatically, and then turn around and do it again the next day. In fact, what we expect of ourselves—and what we let others expect of us—is nothing short of extraordinary.

Our bodies have a natural clock, and our rhythms often match those of the earth itself. If we were to slow down and allow ourselves to lead more even-paced lives that are in balance with the cycles of nature, we'd find that we'd be healthier and happier more of the time.

In truth, we need more vacation and relaxation time; and until we make our well-being and happiness a bigger priority than our monetary goals, we'll always look at our lives and find something lacking. In many countries, four weeks of vacation time is allotted immediately after someone accepts a new position. Unfortunately, in the United States and some other Western countries, most people start with one week of vacation and have to work for several years just to increase to two. This is simply not enough time to get the rejuvenation we need.

If you find yourself in this situation, it's all the more important for you to create mini-vacations within your everyday life. Take at least a few days off periodically, and leave your work behind. Find specific times when you can relax and reclaim your inner sense of peace and well being. By weaving self-care into your hectic lifestyle, you'll project a clear intention for a joyful and magnetic life. So prioritize your own needs, goals, and happiness at least as much as you do others'.

The more of us who choose to be less urgent, create more leisure, and engage in loving and truly connected communication, the more we'll be able to slow down the momentum of this accelerated consciousness and bring greater peace to ourselves and the entire world.

Love or Fear?

Another interesting element in the process of destiny creation is the shared consciousness of the specific groups you belong to. As long as you embrace the beliefs and lifestyle choices of a certain community, you'll be influenced by that shared energy, helping project it out into the world. You may have been taught to behave in a certain way or believe certain things in the past, but now you must choose for yourself. If the collective energy doesn't honor you or bring real value to the planet, then you need to choose to rise above it. When you embrace the pervasive attitude of any group—whatever it may be—your life will be impacted by the force of that pooled attraction. If it's filled with hate or promotes manipulation or fear, then those will be major components of the energy and results that you get back.

Whether it's individually or as a group, you need to know that you contribute to the fields of emotional consciousness that we all share. The two greatest ones are the fields of love and fear. Each and every day you contribute to one or the other by virtue of your thoughts, behaviors, and emotional responses. You'll learn more about the many aspects of shared consciousness throughout the following chapters, but understanding your part in these common fields is an important responsibility.

The power of love isn't just some New Age cliché. It's a very real force in the world—and it has a huge impact on your life and the lives of everyone else. Its absence in your own heart is guaranteed to deplete you, and its presence and intention will empower and enlighten you in more ways than you can ever imagine.

Caring for others as well as yourself expands the energetic field of love in the Universe. This is vitally important to you as an individual and to the entire future of the human race. In terms of shared consciousness, you can't be removed from the influence of what's going on around you. Nor can the world remain unaffected by your daily energy. Every compassionate thought, word, or deed—no matter whom it's directed to—feeds the expansion of loving vibration and returns it to you and everyone else.

Love ignites the power of every law. So choose it, express it, feel it, and intend it for yourself and everyone else. Live in love . . . and your life force will shine!

CHAPTER SIX

SPIRIT CYCLES AND SOUL INTENTIONS

"The creative, spontaneous soul sends forth its promptings of desire and aspiration in us. These promptings are our true fate, which is our business to fulfil."

— D. H. LAWRENCE

Who are you? Where are you from? Is it possible that the truest part of you has somehow gotten lost? Perhaps it fell away when the threads of your reality frayed and there was a tear in your truth.

A Tear in the Truth

Once upon an eternal time, a blindingly brilliant light shined with lofty, loving Consciousness and thought the thoughts of a trillion minds. From the infinite awareness sprang sparkling love, grace, and peace—expanding happiness without measure.

And in the thoughts there were voices that said, "Let us create an expression of ourselves, and a place to experience the wonderful feelings." And the intention for physical life was formed. Over what seemed to be a very long time—but was really just a moment of love—the stage was set with beautiful stars and sparkling waters and places of wonder beyond description. And the thoughts went forward from the love—each one a beautiful beam of beloved light, each one an expression of the grand and brilliant Consciousness, shaped with love and excited to live in this new experience that had been created.

Each light entered the physical plane, experiencing pleasure and adventure, and longing for more. And over time, each began to forget about its light, having only distant memories of the love and brilliant Consciousness from which it came. It needed more and more pleasure because it got very distracted with the body it had—and with the other bodies around it (who were actually lights themselves who had forgotten about their love, too).

With each new experience in this physical place, the memories of the Love Consciousness kept slipping farther and farther away, making the lights long for what was missing and wonder what was wrong.

And each light beam said, "I must find . . . something. There must be something to make me feel better, to make me feel right again."

So all the lights started to look around them, searching for the thing that their inner memories missed.

They looked all around them for love and adventure and pleasure of all kinds; and they found others looking, too. Some of the lights found a few of the things they were looking for, yet deep inside they still felt something was missing. They found some love, but it was nothing compared to the distant memory of their Source. They found some joy, but it paled in comparison to the profound joy they missed. So they continued to look and look for more.

The lights found some pretty rocks in the earth and they used them to barter for the objects they thought would bring them happiness. They discovered things to do that were exciting, and they had moments in their lives where they were able to feel a bit powerful—but nothing like the power they had felt in the light. Whatever they found, it seemed never to be enough, so they kept looking and searching and striving for more.

They gathered together, forming groups that competed for power, glory, and goods. They got so caught up in their searching that they began to believe this was what gave meaning to their lives. They thought they could fill the emptiness with what they might find.

And in their striving, they often found that they got angry and frightened that someone might take away their joy—worried that someone else would find more.

So the lights kept on searching, worrying, and competing—getting farther and farther away from the truth. They totally forgot they were thoughts to begin with and that they still had the love and the light within. If they had just relaxed and stopped looking outside, their gazes would have soon settled on their own beautiful being. The memory of the Love Consciousness that once sent them forth would have been reawakened, and they would have rejoiced in the knowledge that they were already home.

Seeking the Truth

You are eternal spirit. Contrary to what you may imagine, you're not just a spark of soul residing in a physical body. You're fully spirit—as much as you've ever been or will ever be. It may seem strange, but you are—at the same time—fully spirit and fully human, soul and personality, light and substance.

People often find themselves on opposite sides of the fence where this issue is concerned. Some see themselves as only human, and material reality is all there is. Others say that this physical life is just an illusion, a fraudulent experience that doesn't matter at all. Still others believe that although spirit and substance can coexist, the spirit is altered in some way by virtue of that duality. They believe that during the time they're in this plane—in the form of body and soul—their spirit is limited. Their assumption is that when people die, they become more spiritual, but that's not the case. They simply become *less* physical. The release of a body doesn't increase spiritual powers; it just decreases earthly distractions.

This duality can be extremely confusing to our mortal minds, a completely foreign concept in our sense of ourselves. But it's an essential truth that can bring clarity and real power to everything in our lives—especially to our approach to attraction. As long as we refuse to embrace this duality, however, we miss out on an important understanding that could facilitate much of our destiny creation.

This balance of power is just another paradox that earthly existence delivers to us. Physical life may in some ways be a transitory illusion, yet it's also a very certain reality that must be dealt with. At the same time, spiritual life is true and powerful, yet it's an unseen reality, an ethereal force that's hard to define. When we work on developing a higher awareness of our spiritual truth, we find much greater clarity in the human experience. Spirit-centered life makes the material world more meaningful, and the connection empowers us beyond measure.

Your eternal self is a strong influence on your process of attraction. You may not realize it, but this identity lives within you and expresses itself through you in countless ways. Your soul has its own never-ending consciousness; and through this it reveals your truth, power, and higher intentions. It's this last piece, your soul's intention and your spirit's purpose, that's a significant—but often hidden—factor in all that happens to you. This mysterious component can create a lot of confusion about what's going on. After all, your soul may have an entirely different agenda from anything your mortal mind has ever thought of.

The Choices of Spirit

The Universe is unlimited, a vast playground for the spirit to explore. The choice to experience life on the physical plane must be compelling indeed! In order to fully understand why your journey has taken a certain direction, it's helpful to know what your soul's motivation may be. There are five main reasons why spirit chooses to come here. Knowing what has driven you to this earthly adventure can help immensely in your personal evolution and self-empowerment.

1. Your Spirit Longs to Express Itself

If sometimes you want to shout from the rooftops who you are—or even *that* you are—don't be surprised. It may just be your soul longing to break into self-recognition and joyous expression. Your eternal spirit knows the worth and value that lives within you during every moment of your life. Your soul vibrates with this self-awareness and Divine acknowledgment, and the desire to celebrate that and share it on this plane is one of your compelling reasons for being here. To aid that self-expression, there's the vastly exciting prospect of soul creativity.

There's a creative spark that lives within the heart of each and every one of us, and at some time we can feel this expressive need well up within. It may or may not manifest as something artistic, but whatever it might be, this is a very real part of our spirits' earthly motivations—and a compelling factor in our earthly desires. It's the longing to express something that's uniquely our own; and whether it's in the form of discovery, beauty, or value, it can bring significant meaning and fulfillment to us and to others. Opening up to creative inspiration can go a long way in healing the rift between mind and soul, allowing us to reconnect with our spirit in profound inspiration. It can also help align our spirit's intentions with our personal dreams, a connection that truly accelerates our magnetic attraction.

Soulution

What do you want to express that you may have been holding inside? Write about it; talk to a friend. Express yourself down to your soul.

Is there something you've been longing to create, perhaps to discover or even build? Think about how you can be more creative—and more spontaneous. When your soul calls you to do so, you'll find it hard to resist. Let your spirit be the composer in your life, and find out what magical music it can make.

2. Your Spirit Longs to Experience

Think about the times you've been in one location but have thought longingly of another. It may seem unlikely, but your soul knows that sensation, too. Although there's much to do in the spirit world—including service, assistance, and inspiration—it must be acknowledged that there's a great deal to do on this earthly plane as well. In fact, physical sensations can be very compelling. Even spirit can long to breathe the air, see a sunset, or feel a warm breeze or cool water.

As you'll see when you explore the phenomena of karma and reincarnation, some people spend entire lifetimes driven by the desire for physical experience. When attachments are formed, the need becomes great. The desire for food, sex, alcohol, narcotics, excitement, or virtually anything on the physical plane can cause a being to return time after time with that particular experie as their central motivation. This can also be a significant factor in destiny creation.

You can become attached to just about anything—the people you're with, the activities you like to do, and the body sensations that give you pleasure. This attachment can lead to addictions in the physical world, creating a very compelling drive for incarnation in order to continue the experience. As you move deeper into attachment and longing, your soul will need to learn an important lesson—to reprioritize and let go.

SOULUTION

Enjoy the experiences of your life with gusto and appreciation. If you find yourself becoming addicted or overattached, then the experiences are actually moving you away from spirit and increasing your sense of lack. This will disturb synchronicity and block your attraction—only causing you to long to escape even more.

Ask yourself what course of action would honor you, then muster up the courage to take it. Balance is the key, and until you achieve it, you'll find yourself returning to that lesson over and over again. As much as your spirit desires any earthly thing, it wants self-mastery more.

The soul believes that lessons are a compelling part of eternal life, and it supports your path of learning. In fact, this is one of your biggest motivations for journeying to the physical world. Whatever the situation, it's always a valuable choice to stop and reflect, *What does my soul want me to know, do, or learn?*

3. Your Spirit Longs to Learn and Grow

While the ego and personality tend to resist change, the spirit embraces it. In fact, personal evolution is a big motivation for your soul's earthly choices. Like the beam of light that's separated from its Source and seeks solutions elsewhere, your individual identity can get seriously bogged down in personal dilemmas of self-doubt, longing, and fear. This loss of eternal memory invariably leads to the sense that something is missing, which can drive you toward material acquisition.

Yet the spirit unceasingly calls all of us to remember our Source, to recall that there's so much more. For many of us, this realization is, in itself, the big life lesson—to let go of the incessant striving, redefine what's really valuable, and then prioritize that. For others, there are equally important lessons, such as genuine self-love, self-valuing, and compassion for other people. Just as water always seeks its own level, love, compassion, and value are spirit's natural state. When the personality is out of sync with that, we'll unavoidably move in the direction of learning. The soul's purpose will be found in higher intentions, and our material goals may have to take a backseat.

Through the many experiences of your life, your soul will continually lead you toward healing, understanding, and resolution. You may go through vastly different cycles of learning, or you may face one major lesson with a significant theme that repeats itself. Until you master it, the opportunity for growth will keep reappearing. Whether in the form of a difficulty or a blessing, the lessons you're presented with must be learned. And in terms of your spirit, your eternal truth, power, and value are always the solutions.

*Soul*ution

What are the patterns in the problems you've faced? What are the lessons that keep popping up? Some of the most common are:

- *Choosing self-love*
- *Surrendering attachment*
- *Living with compassion*
- *Letting go of fear*

Learning your lessons and honoring the purpose of your soul will help put you in Universal flow. So find out what you need to know or do, and create the intention to live in a way that prioritizes it. Bring your God consciousness to it! Affirm its power and make it a real force in your life. You owe it to yourself to learn your spirit's truth and bring that grand point of view to all that you do.

4. Your Spirit Wants You to Awaken to Your Sacred Identity

One of our most significant truths is our eternal Source and identity. This spiritual presence isn't a sideshow to life—it's the main event, and it should *not* be overlooked. Most of us are too busy to give it much thought, but our essential nature is so intrinsic to our being and strength that ignoring it would be a huge oversight. In fact, this is the core power of our life; and when embraced, it can change everything.

The presence of the soul needs to be addressed. You can deny it now and still make some success for yourself, yet at some point in time, the search for spirit—or at least meaning—is likely to call to you and make its importance known.

Unfortunately, it's often through discomfort that the drive back to Source becomes a priority. When you experience a loss so deep that you have nowhere else to go, you'll turn to spiritual understanding. When you're at the end of your life and you find yourself wondering what it was all for, you'll seek—and yearn for—a higher meaning.

But it isn't necessary to wait for unhappiness or old age. You can heighten your awareness of your loving Source right now. You can find a higher meaning for everything—both good and bad—within your eternal viewpoint and your ever-present connection to the Divine. This is an option that's always available to you. Stop and consider your relationship to all things. Feel the whispers of eternity within each breath. In all that you experience, the power starts here.

Soulution

Love is Source Consciousness, and there's authentic power in reawakening to it. Nothing needs to take you away from that, whether it's joy, difficulty, or the distractions of daily life. Your spirit will always seek its all-loving Source, and it will either nudge you or compel you in that direction through the vagaries of your life.

Dialogue with your higher self; meditate on the presence of Divine love in your own center. By opening your heart and mind to this awareness now—in whatever form your belief may take—you'll find a growing sense of clarity, peace, and understanding that will empower and support you in everything you do.

5. Your Spirit Longs to Love and Serve

As part of its Divine expression, there's a personal path that's more attractive to your soul than any other in this earthly experience: love and service. Since the soul remembers its Source—and longs to connect with it at every turn—expressing and experiencing love in this realm will always be a priority that comes from within. In addition, this fluid, brilliant, caring energy is the most creative and healing force in the Universe. As a result, your soul will repeatedly make this its highest intention.

Your spirit is inextricably connected to the joys and plights of every other soul on the planet; and what happens to others can't be separated from what happens to you. Balance, peace, and harmony are the natural order of things in the spirit realm, and your soul longs to bring these energies to you and to the entire earth.

It's only the ego that seeks power through competition and conflict, only the needy personality that's driven to divide instead of unite. In the ongoing struggle to compensate for the loss of Source connection, the ego makes desperate attempts at false empowerment and superficial gain. But deep within the heart of each one of us, the soul is able to see the souls of others; and when it does, its most profound intention is to love and serve.

SOULUTION

The soul's desire to heal and unite is as intrinsic to your eternal being as blood is to your body, so when you align your own intention with this lofty goal, you bring healing to yourself and unity to your own scattered energy. By expanding the love of your eternal Source, you connect with the Universe in stunning attraction and dynamic vibration. Your life force resonates at the highest level of experience—your eternal truth. And from that true place, the intention to serve accelerates the love that we all share.

Service doesn't have to mean huge sacrifices. There are many little things that you can do to share compassionate energy with others. Begin with a smile, a compliment, a favor, or merely a caring thought. Start today, and your soul will continue leading the way.

When you're ready, add greater intentions of service to your life. In the unity of all things, what you do for another, you do for yourself. Give your time, your love, and your compassion. You, your spirit, and the entire Universe will be pleased.

Spiritual Split

Service is one way to bridge the gap in your spirit/human duality. But even greater understanding is needed to heal this schism of experience. Your eternal soul has its own intention—and it comes to this life with a guiding directive to prioritize that intention, even though you may not be aware yet of exactly what it is. In fact, your soul's purpose may not easily align with your ego's focus, and this disconnect between higher motivation and personal desire is one of the big dilemmas where the laws of attraction are concerned.

Your soul definitely has the intention to achieve something—although it's usually not related to money. It may plan to heal old hurts, yet your ego could be driven to get revenge for them. Your soul may be intending to expand love and unity; but your ego may be compelled to compete, acquire, and gain power over others. Your spirit's greatest joy may be to bring truth, understanding, and honoring to you and others; yet you may firmly believe that your greatest personal joy would be to make more money and achieve more material success.

What happens when you're faced with such a schism of direction? In this conflicting state, it's no wonder that you can become confused about your purpose and get frustrated over the seeming lack of results. When the desires of your ego and spirit are at odds, the opposing intentions can play havoc with your life force and have a dramatic impact on what you'll attract.

Your solution starts by developing an awareness of what your soul's intention may be. I'll address this issue in greater depth when I talk about life lessons, but it would be helpful now to start examining the repeated patterns of your life in order to see what your soul may have in mind. You probably have at least a few lessons to learn. How deeply do you love yourself? How strong is your connection to Source? Are you here to experience, to express and create, or to love and serve?

Spirit Cycles and Shared Consciousness

Throughout your life, you'll go through many cycles that are driven by your spirit. Seasons of learning, loving, experiencing, and creating—all of these can be driven by your soul's intent. But your soul isn't alone in its drive to achieve a higher purpose.

Just as there's a consciousness shared by individuals, there's a group spirit consciousness as well. The experiences that we go through together often reveal a major intention of our collective spirits. Our souls join in a desire for transformation; and that can lead families, community groups, countries, and even the whole world in important directions.

You may, in fact, be feeling the momentum of a shared spirit cycle in your own life. Many recent global changes—especially in the economy—have shown that none of us can continue living according to the patterns and habits of the past. There are important messages being revealed about the need to change our priorities and be clearer about what brings value into our lives. This realization has been so dramatic in the lives of so many people that it can no longer be resisted.

Part of that realization has to do with money. We've been living for too long with a major schism in our approach to it. On the one hand, we tend to prioritize it more than anything else. It's what we strive for and even dedicate our lives to. On the other hand, we've spent too many years hardly valuing it at all. We overspend, buying things we don't need and never use, throwing money away on meaningless mementoes that we rarely think about again.

Our common spirit intention isn't going to allow this polarization to go on any longer. The message is clear: We need to prioritize money less, while we value and appreciate it more! We need to reduce the striving and prioritize the other sources of value in our life—love; relationships; laughter; leisure time; relaxation; and qualities such as integrity, grace, and compassion.

We're in a shared cycle of growth and transformation, and it's compelling us to change. We need to wake up the soul; focus on real value; and cast out our demons of desperation, envy, jealousy, and fear. When we do, we'll go a long way toward healing ourselves and our suffering. And we'll finally be able to achieve prosperity of the spirit—peaceful appreciation and abiding love.

Your life is eternal, and this earthly incarnation is just the blink of an eye when compared to your spiritual existence. In the long run, the Universe will prioritize your soul's intention over your ego's earthly desires. Your spirit doesn't really care if you're rich or poor, as long as its higher intentions are met. But when you make it a priority to love, learn, and live with reverence, the Universe will prioritize your personal goals as well.

So it's helpful to look at your life and ask yourself, *What am I really here to do?* Whether it's raising your children with love or finally learning how to honor and value yourself, the answer you get will probably have more meaning than merely making money. There's nothing wrong with amassing a fortune, but it will be much easier to do—and much more fulfilling—if you can accomplish it in conjunction with your soul's deepest longings and expansive love.

CHAPTER SEVEN

CYCLES OF LIFE

"In the midst of winter, I finally learned that there was in me an invincible summer."

— ALBERT CAMUS

It's clear that many factors contribute to destiny creation. Of primary consideration, of course, is how you activate the laws with your consciousness, energy, and intention. Yet as you've seen, these things aren't always the source of the vast array of your experiences. And although you may not be able to identify the causes for every single event, when you look at things more objectively—and open yourself to learning your spirit's intentions—you can more easily identify where you are and where you're going next.

Life is a process, a series of cycles—ups and downs, activity and quiet, beginnings and endings. When you can recognize and define the cycle you're in, you're free to use your personal powers to transform any situation.

These natural seasons of the human experience are bound to happen. In fact, they're one of the major influences on destiny creation. It's the ability to go through the different periods with power and grace that determines the quality of your life. In order to move forward, however, you need to know where you are. It's like trying to find a place you've never been to: you may have a map showing your destination, yet if you don't know where you are now, you'll never be able to get started and keep going in the right direction.

This is true with your life as well. If you're going to move on to the next cycle—to your next experience—you need to understand exactly where you are. By beginning to understand what you're learning now, you can maximize that energy and use the power of your consciousness and intention to shift it in the direction you desire.

Transformers

At this time in history, many people are in the process of transformation. This *growth cycle* may even involve major changes, including such extremes as marriage, divorce, severe illness, unexpected reversals, and even death and rebirth. Any type of transformation—whether physical, emotional, financial, or regarding a relationship—may be difficult to experience. Yet many of these extremes often lead to momentous growth and personal achievement, even though the hardship may seem unbearable at the time.

You shouldn't blame yourself or focus on faultfinding during difficult situations. If you're involved in a series of changes, let yourself identify the shifts and look for the messages. Finding problems with yourself will only increase your resistence to creating something new. This will stop the transformation in its tracks, and you'll just have to go through something similar again in order to make the change complete.

Look at the cycles in nature. Winter is a cold and barren time, yet the earth doesn't blame itself for that. As bleak as that season can be, it's also a time of quiet regeneration, where nature sleeps and readies itself for becoming new again. Each season allows the process to continue. Winter is nature going inward and slowing down. Spring is a time of new birth. Summer is the season of growth, and fall is the cycle of harvesting that which has been sown.

The human life experience is similar, including physical transformation, birth, puberty, aging, and death—with many, many changes in between. It's important to know, however, that change brings new potential, and there's never a death without a rebirth. Difficulty doesn't have to cause us to lose our power. If we use each cycle to the best of our ability, the end of one experience can open up to the dawn of a beautiful new era.

Cycles of Expansion

Most people love their times of expansion. Things seem to accelerate, bringing greater and greater results. You can get swept up in the momentum of things; there's more to do, more to see, more to experience.

Cycles of expansion are times of increase. Sometimes that means more money, but finances aren't the only things that flourish. Families expand when children are born, and businesses grow when new projects are created. In these and many other cases, the effort amplifies as well.

Whatever the increase, remember to be very conscious of the opportunities it brings. Sometimes when you get busy, it's easy to stop reflecting, but don't let yourself get consumed by the growth. It's a great chance to help extend your awareness and insight as well. So open up to the new and varied experiences and consider how you can use them as a part of your personal process. Never assume that this expansive time defines or completes you. It is you who defines this experience—and all others.

In a time of monetary expansion, you can sit back and reap your rewards, but don't be lulled into inactivity and overindulgence. Live in appreciation and be sure to value all the aspects of your life—not just the new goodies that may be coming to you. It might be that this period of increase will last awhile, but even if it does, you want to be solidly established in your inner sense of well-being, not just attached to externals.

Nothing expands forever—the Universe is always changing. The economy corrects itself, and highs are followed by lows—sometimes to great extremes. Times of abundant harvest can be followed by drought and famine. Climate, money, cultures, and individuals all have periods of expansion, but they don't last indefinitely. The great Roman Empire thrived and grew for hundreds of years, spreading across continents, but even it was brought down by tribes of barbarians.

Personal patterns have similar highs and lows, and your own life cycles may be many and varied. There are times of great change that expand your joys immensely. There are seasons of significant losses that transform you and move you forward. And between those extremes, you may find yourself in prolonged periods where things don't seem to change at all.

Cycles of Perpetuation

Sometimes it seems as though things are pretty much staying the same, and the status quo may last for quite some time. This is the cycle of perpetuation, an energetic momentum of repetition and continuation. During such periods, you may find some changes, but basic elements are maintained in such a way that it seems as though nothing remarkable is taking place. Be on notice, however: there's always something going on under the surface.

Periods of perpetuation may be idyllic—pleasant times with happy episodes strung together by normal tasks. Enjoying lifelong relationships and spending decades in the same career can be wonderful, but depending on your approach, they may also be long spells of tedious work and joyless activities. These stretches of time seem to be innocuous enough, but they can often be the path of least resistance. You might tend to stay in a marriage, a job, or another situation not because it's nurturing, but merely because it seems like the easiest thing to do.

Be careful not to perpetuate something that dishonors you. It only digs you deeper into a negative pattern that then becomes your way of life. Instead of you being in charge, the momentum of your habits holds sway over you. As a result, it's very important in this (and every) cycle to bring your consciousness to bear.

A cycle of perpetuation may be totally healthy, however. If the people you're with and what you're doing honor you, enjoy it. Use the time to expand your interests and explore life-enhancing activities. This interval may be a gift from the Universe, allowing you to add things such as meditation, journaling, and affirmation to your daily repertoire. These activities can be very important if the momentum of your life takes any problematic turns, so establishing them during a time of comfort is a great choice.

Analyze your status quo. If you find that you're perpetuating something that dishonors you, such as an addiction or an abusive relationship, it's time to stop and take charge. Living in long periods of negative perpetuation can radically affect what you attract. Alcoholism, gambling, sex addiction, and untold unhealthy patterns can virtually eat up your entire life. When that's the case, it's up to you to decide to break the pattern and move on to your next cycle: transformation.

Cycles of Transformation

You're a transformer, and you can change according to the wisdom each experience may bring. Knowing this, you can rest assured that any major shift always brings with it a multitude of feelings. Marriage, divorce, the birth of a child, the loss of a job—all of these are significant times of transformation, eliciting emotions that are both positive and negative. So whatever you may be going through now, try to remember that it can lead to value, learning, and personal power. The old will always give way to the new; and if you choose, you'll be able to revitalize yourself and arrive at the new place with greater power and understanding.

Some transformations are so extreme that they change the very ways in which you define yourself. When something happens that's so harrowing that you can no longer engage in the same old activities or connect with the same old people, you're forced to then take an entirely different path. In these times, you must not only change your process, you must sometimes also revise your purpose—and even change how you perceive yourself. This is especially true if your old self-definitions were largely formed through the pursuits that are passing away.

After all, if you define yourself through a relationship and that relationship dies—or if your identity is based on your career and you're suddenly laid off—what happens to your self-view then? In such cases, you're dealt a double difficulty, for you're not only facing the unknown about your future, you're in the same situation with yourself. This can be monumentally challenging on both levels. First, you can lose your sense of stability and safety, unsure of which direction to go next. Second, you lose your inner sense of yourself, as well as your certainty about who you are and what matters to you most.

Such cycles of transformation force you to let go of the old ways of doing business. When something in your life changes dramatically, it's often because the lesson is so profound that the old ways just don't fit anymore. Often the very purpose of transformation is to arrive at a better place—or a better process.

There are some people who seem to have hardship upon hardship with not much relief in between. Others seem to have their entire lives built around one major problem, whether it's poverty, illness, or isolation. These types of experiences are even more powerful transformations, for they indicate lives of *initiation.*

A life of initiation can be so severe that it seems totally overwhelming. Yet this is the spirit's opportunity to do something extremely powerful—in healing or evolving on a personal level, or even in inspiring on a global one. This path can be truly important because it can take you to an entirely different place in your eternal process.

These difficult, "shaken to the core" losses can actually bring forth wonderful blessings. They offer you the chance to reinvent and redefine yourself—both in terms of your daily life and your spiritual reality. There's a great gift in the risk of releasing your old external definitions and finding your truth in this far deeper place. In fact, living with spirit as the core of your truth is so important that it gives you meaning and support in any type of situation.

Yet the depth of catastrophe may be the only time that you allow yourself to seriously consider a higher meaning. This is unfortunate, because making your spiritual understanding a way of life could reduce so much stress and accelerate so much strength. You don't have to wait for difficulty or disaster to force you to face this ever-present, soul-centered option. Every cycle of life is seen more clearly through the lens of eternity.

SOULUTION

You have an identity that preexisted whatever dark times you may go through. The truth is this: you are spirit first, one who has come to this earth plane for a wide variety of personal experiences. In your heart, you're unruffled, undeterred, and unafraid. Your spirit sees the eternal as real—and any dark cycle as merely the passing of a difficult day in the long span of a beautiful, infinite life. Every experience is part of a far bigger reality, and your soul can help you with whatever must be dealt with.

Step back and look at things from a longer point of view. Let go of the fear and urgency, and open up to your spirit's capacity to face life with willingness and peace. Meditate on the real meaning of the experience. Trust that no matter what, you do have the power to handle things. And with your soul's assistance, your choice to transform will lead you in a far better direction.

New Direction

This soul-centered shift is just the first liberating aspect of major transformation. In addition to this spiritual awakening, periods of critical change can also give you the opportunity to redirect your earthly experience. As hard as it may be to deal with at the time, the end of one thing will always mean the beginning of another, and it's important to process the experience and to the eventual opportunities. When you're forc go and live in trust, this can lead to unexpected places and wonderful outcomes.

I have had many difficult and significant periods of transformation myself. One particular time was so horrible that I've never shared the story publicly before. It happened when I was a high-school teacher and I was staying late one day to grade finals. I didn't realize it at the time, but other than the janitor, whose office was at the other side of the building, I was the only person around. I was just about to pack up my things when a former student came in—one who'd developed an unsavory reputation. I started to walk away, but before I knew it, he attacked me. In a moment's time, he had me pinned to the desk with a knife at my throat. When he started unbuttoning my shirt, I didn't know what to do; he had me immobilized, and I could feel the blood trickling down my neck where the knife was piercing my skin.

I was truly blessed and protected, however. Before it went any further, another former student came in and sent my attacker running. I seemed fine, but I was shaken up so much that it changed my life.

Except for a scratch at the throat, I was physically unhurt. But emotionally I felt damaged to the core. If that other student hadn't come in, I know for certain I would have been raped, and it's very likely that I could have been killed. That realization shattered my trust in others, destroyed my love for my profession, and made me doubt my own judgment. I was so deeply changed that I knew I'd have to quit teaching.

I had no idea what I was going to do next—I'd been teaching for seven years, and my education and certification was in that area. Yet I wouldn't even consider going back. I knew that I would no longer be honoring myself if I remained in that environment, so I soon found that I had to deal with two traumas: that of the experience itself, as well as the ordeal of losing that definition of myself (not to mention that source of income).

This was a huge upheaval for me. Luckily, I have a totally different perspective now, but at the time I felt as though my world was collapsing. I had wanted to be a teacher my entire life. From childhood through college, that was the career I had focused on. It wasn't just a job to me; it was a profession that I enjoyed, found challenging, and was proud of.

Yet all of a sudden I had to abandon all of that. I had to let go of that identity and the lifestyle that had become my daily reality. Instead, I was faced with moving out into the unknown and rediscovering who I was and what I wanted to do next.

I went through several different jobs, none of which was a real fit. I was unhappy, struggling to find something that would resonate with me. Yet as horrible as that time was, I'm now certain beyond any doubt that the whole experience was a blessing for me. It was then that I dove into spiritual studies—taking classes in meditation, self-hypnosis, and even mind and intention programming. I visualized myself going to a job that I enjoyed and felt fulfilled by—even though I had no idea what that job would be. I relaxed, let go of the striving, and took the time to heal both the trauma and the transition. I also worked diligently on my personal and spiritual development.

In time, I was led into the field of counseling. I found that I was fascinated and exhilarated by the process. I loved my clients, and it wasn't long before I began public speaking, which to me was another form of teaching. And it was this newfound profession that eventually led me to where I am today. I'd experienced the death of a career, but in time that death created wonderful new opportunities that wouldn't have appeared if it weren't for that very difficult time of transformation.

Time for a Change

A lot of people have gone through—and *are* going through—difficult shifts. Something happens to change their reality in a truly profound way, and although it may seem unbearable at the time, they're able to look back on it with clarity and even appreciation.

This may seem like small consolation to you if you're in the throes of a life-altering cycle right now, but it's important to remember the growth that comes through transformation—and the beginning that comes with ending.

In Chapter 9, I'll be talking more about how to break through these cycles and arrive at a better place. But remember, there's real power in transformation. When you bring your consciousness and intention to it, you can shift realities and push through even the most difficult of times.

SOULUTION

The cycles of life are a natural part of the human experience. You signed up for them when you came on this earthly journey, so use each one as a bridge to something greater—not just in the material world, but in your heart, mind, habits, and reactions.

No matter what cycle you're in, ask yourself the following questions. Write the answers in your journal.

- *What's the lesson my spirit may have in mind for this experience?*
- *What kind of thoughts and beliefs can I choose to empower me through this?*
- *What action can I take to get the most out of this experience and help move me forward?*

In everything in life, it's your response that determines whether you or the event has more power. Whatever may be going on, affirm your ability to redefine and rise above it—and your willingness to cycle through.

Whatever you're going through—whether it's getting out of debt, finding or healing a relationship, or dealing with something physical—it's all a part of your personal evolution. You have to be patient, persistent, and self-aware. If you don't understand the process, y give up. But remember, if you're given the o transform and you refuse, that option is likely to show up again—and in an equally interesting way.

The I Ching, the ancient text of divination written nearly 5,000 years ago, offers advice on how to deal with difficulty. In Hexagram 39, called Obstruction, it says that during the time of obstruction, "The superior man turns his attention to himself and molds his character." This clearly demonstrates an important purpose for hard times: Go within and find a new and deeper meaning—and a more authentic power. Meditate on the issue and take your ego out of the mix. In your introspection, you'll be able to achieve stunning moments of enlightenment, trust, and clarity of perception that will transcend your temporary concerns and support you forever.

Don't wait until a problem is resolved before you look for joy. Life is in a constant state of change, and if you believe that everything has to be settled before you can be happy, you may be waiting for a very long time. Find joy in the moment and accept the uncertainty. Be in the bliss of letting go.

Each season of your life is a part of your eternal process. It's what you do with the energy of that cycle that determines both the quality of your life and results of that experience. Always remember that there are both internal and external results. As you continue to go within, you renew your strength and your spirit. When you shift your inner life, you'll not only transform your outer life, you will also change the nature of the world itself.

CHAPTER EIGHT

KARMIC CYCLES

"Consciousness is [the] inner light kindled in the soul . . . a music, strident or sweet, made by the friction of existence."

— GEORGE SANTAYANA

Like the cycles of your personal life, your eternal life has cycles, too. Your soul has a much longer view than your personality does, seeing this incarnation as somewhat fleeting yet very purposeful. In terms of attraction and destiny creation, an important influence is your spirit's specific plans.

We know that soul intentions drive the spirit to an earthly incarnation. There are periods of bliss and blues, sorrow and service, love and learning—a vast array of experiences stimulated by the soul's intent. This can go on for many lifetimes—and between lives as well.

Some people have a difficult time believing in reincarnation, but if you look at the principles of energy and matter, it really makes a lot of sense. Matter breaks down, but energy transmutes; and although it may change form, it doesn't end.

Your eternal soul is like that. You start as spirit energy, then assume physical form, maintaining the spiritual energy all the while. When the part of you that was physical passes on, your spiritual energy remains, taking with it the information that was encoded into your personal and eternal consciousness. As a result, many of the things you're experiencing today originated in previous lifetimes and were brought forward for you and your soul to work on together.

Every life is a part of your soul's evolution, a part of your eternal identity's process. When you come into this life, you may forget your Divine Source, but you don't lose your spiritual information. Instead, you add and record present events along with new data into your soul's storehouse of experience. Every experience—from this life and others—becomes encoded into your eternal consciousness. This is often (but not always) why you're brought together with the people you encounter and why you experience the life situations you do.

Tracking Your Karma Code

Many people are confused by the concept of karma. They think it's a form of punishment for some unknown wrongdoing in a potentially frightening history. Karma, however, is all about energy. It's not punishment; it's a return of the energy you've put out in the past, resurfacing so that you have an opportunity to experience it yourself. Karma isn't the Universe sentencing you to some horrible payback. It's your eternal soul's choice to find out how certain energies feel—and an opportunity to experience the emotions that you've caused yourself and others to feel in the past.

Karma is so complex that it needs extensive exploration, and I'm going to expand on this topic in much more detail in my next book. But it's important to review here because karma is a major influence on the people and experiences you attract. As such, it's a very real energetic force in your life. Along with the energy of the laws, life cycles, shared consciousness, and other spirit cycles, it's a major factor in your destiny creation.

While a lot of your karmic path is set up for learning, there are other intentions that your soul may have for its karmic choices. In fact, there may be big plans that you're not even aware of. Like a parent with a child, the spirit knows what's really important. The child may want the latest toy, and the parent may indulge him. But the parent, like the soul, knows that there will be a time to move on to more important things.

Karma is a part of that. Your eternal life has more meaning than can be perceived in terms of this life alone. So it's helpful to know what may have transpired in the past and why that has a bearing on what's going on now. There are three main reasons for the karmic patterns your soul picks: repetition, compensation, and "retribution." Let's take a look at how these may be factoring into your life experiences.

1. Karmic Repetition

The soul longs to experience, and what it likes to experience, it likes to repeat. Part of what draws the soul to earthly incarnation in the first place is the experience of physicality. The taste of eating, the joy of sex, the lightheaded feelings of alcohol—all of these sensations can be quite compelling. Our blissful reactions to these and many other things become encoded into our eternal consciousness, and can be a driving force when we decide what we'd like to experience in this life.

Have you ever taken to something right away and felt quite natural in the experience? It may be that you've had a karmic connection with that activity. If you take up a sport or even an instrument and it's a breeze from the beginning, chances are you've played it in a past life. If you find that learning a certain language is easy for you, you could have spoken it in a previous incarnation. And if you experience the phenomenon known as *love at first sight,* you can pretty much guarantee that you've been in love with that person before.

While it's easy to see why we'd want to repeat some things in our lives, it's important to know that this drive for repetition can also create some problems where karma is concerned. It can also be a compelling force in our destiny creation—and not always in a good way.

Oftentimes, current addictions (very real obstacles to attraction) can find their source in karmic patterns of repetition. For example, if you're having problems with alcoholism now, you may have been an alcoholic in a past life, and that drive for pleasure and escapism may be deeply encoded in your desires. If you were a compulsive gambler in a past life, your soul may have renewed that compulsion now—either from the desire to experience it or the desire to heal it. In fact, any pattern you feel stuck in could be a result of karmic repetition—and knowing that can help you get unstuck and move on.

This is true for relationships, too. You may be with the same person you've been with many times before. It may be a joyous bond or an unhealthy one, but even so, the longing to repeat may keep you there. Healthy, happy relationships are safe places for two souls to work on their lessons together. In dishonoring unions, however, that's not the case.

Why would we repeat addictions and difficult relationships? Often it's because we're driven (and held) by what's familiar to us. *But just as often, it's because we're destined to repeat until we learn to let go. In fact, in the human experience, learning to detach is one of our primary objectives.*

This was the case for a client named Cally who recently contacted me for a past-life regression. She was in a relationship that had made her unhappy, yet she found it very difficult to move on. She'd broken up with this critical man on three occasions, but she consistently found herself going back whenever he called. As we investigated her beliefs and her energy around this relationship experience, we found that there were two sources of her inability to leave.

One was the fact that she'd never really gotten the approval and affection she sought from her father. Her dad had always been unavailable, so she repeatedly picked emotionally unavailable men in order to replay that experience, hopefully with a different, more positive outcome. This is a very common phenomenon. There's an old saying that we marry our parents, and this is the reason why:

we look for the same personality type because we want to resolve old feelings and unfinished business. Unfortunately, the resolution rarely comes about.

But trying to heal her unfinished dad issues wasn't the only reason for Cally to feel stuck in this relationship. She'd been in similar situations with equally noncommittal men, but she always had the strength to walk away before. In this case, however, there was also a compelling karmic connection that kept her returning to this man. Her previous life with him was at a time in history when single women had very few personal resources. In that life, she'd become this man's mistress, and he kept promising that he'd marry her and provide her with riches. Instead of that, though, he continued to give her the barest minimum of support, always promising more but never following through. In that life, she felt stuck, not having any skills, options, or family to turn to. She encoded into her eternal consciousness: *I have to stay. I don't have any options.*

Things were entirely different this time around, however. She was financially independent and capable of providing for herself. Yet that encoded demand, *I have to stay,* continued to be an undercurrent of directing energy, even though she wasn't aware of why she felt that way.

All of this information was very revealing to her on two important levels. First, and most important, she realized that she must stop seeking her father's approval in her romantic relationships. Instead, she must become the source of unconditional love and approval for herself. Second, she realized that she did have the power to let go. The subtle but nagging attachment had been an old, encoded karmic memory. But understanding and working on both of these things made it easier to move on.

Cally now knew why she'd felt so stuck. She did the karmic-release meditations, journaling, and affirmations that appear throughout this chapter; and she was able to shift that energy. She also knew that something very important was happening in terms of her self-esteem and self-valuing. It was time for her to forge a strong sense of her real self-worth—to let go of the lies that her father's dismissal taught her and to start living in—and believing—her own truth.

She wrote out a new, self-empowering definition of herself; and she affirmed that every day. She set boundaries and made self-honoring choices that prioritized and empowered her. She realized that until she established genuine self-love as a way of life, she'd only have to repeat the lesson over and over again. And she didn't want to engage in the old kind of relationship—with herself or others—any longer.

Any pattern of repetition can be transformed. It's so easy to become addicted to alcohol, food, sex, gambling, drugs, or even relationships, for the initial thrills can be irresistible. However, when a pattern becomes destructive or dishonoring, you know it's time to clear that code out of your consciousness.

You may feel needy—or even codependent—in a relationship; you may feel as though you just can't live without your substance of choice. But your eternal truth is absolute: *You are all that you need!* And no matter what negative pattern you may have, when you turn to your own innate power and value, you'll no longer need to repeat the unhealthy habits from this or any other life.

Soulution

If you notice yourself in a habit of overattachment such as eating, drinking, gambling, or relationship codependency, you may be in a lifetime of repetition or compensation. In spite of what your personal desires are, the underlying intentions of this life are to find authentic power within and to heal these excessive attachments.

Meditate on the issue. Visualize the object of your attachment drifting away on the clouds. Bless it and let it go, knowing that you have the power now. Use the following affirmations often, and support them with the self-honoring choices and behavioral changes that are necessary. Ask spirit's help and muster up your courage and eternal strength. You can do it!

Releasing and Empowering Affirmations

- *I release any negative habits that may have resulted from past-life needs.*
- *I am strong, and free to choose what is healthy for me now.*
- *I release any unhealthy attachment to* [name the substance or person here]. *I am clear, empowered, and courageous!*
- *I have power in all of my present choices.*
- *I lead a healthy, balanced life.*

- *The strength of my eternal soul guides me. I am strong, and willing to let go and walk a higher path.*

2. Karmic Compensation

Another karmic path that can lead to unhealthy behaviors and addictions is the need for compensation. Karmic compensation comes from the desire to *reverse* the energy of past experiences. If circumstances were extreme in a past life, a strong desire for compensation may cause them to go in the opposite direction this time around. Like repetition, this can lead to excessive reactions.

For example, if you lived through the potato famine in Ireland, you may have been perpetually hungry, never getting enough to eat. That constant hunger and longing for food would then be encoded into your consciousness. In this life, you could still be driven by that hunger; and since you have plenty of access to food, you could find yourself overeating yet never really feeling satisfied. This life then could become burdened with a weight problem—with your frustration about being overweight turning into resentment for food and a sense of powerlessness about it. Those emotions could also become encoded, swinging you back into another life of deprivation where you would be hungry all over again!

Balance and self-empowerment are key. Establish a strong, sane, and centered approach to all that you long for and all that you resist. Make choices that come from healthy consideration—not habit. When you get off the emotional roller coaster, you'll be able to attract equally healthy people and situations for all the right reasons.

Keep in mind that karmic compensation can also come in the form of relationship issues. For example, if you've been hurt in the past, you may have encoded a conclusion that love is unsafe for you. You may now be living according to that code, wondering why you're not attracting anyone. And if you're feeling that way about a present situation, be aware! Remember that whether it's past or present, you have the option to change fear-based beliefs and encode trust and self-empowerment instead. You don't want your love frustrations in this life to cause you to take vows of celibacy next time—or do you?

It may sound extreme—and a little funny—but this is karmic compensation. Your highly charged experiences create emotions of desire or dread—and you follow those emotions with strong intentions to reverse the situation. This creates a seesaw of energy patterns that are often based in two very opposite drives—excessive longing or profound resistance. But you do have the power to deal with both!

SOULUTION

Your all-or-nothing patterns of attraction will stop when you bring a higher level of consciousness to the extremes of your life—especially those that are highly charged with emotion. Release persistent attachments and false conclusions, and take your power back. Acknowledge your strength in the present moment and your freedom from any influence of the past. Affirm: I release the need to compensate for any problems of the past. I am safe, balanced, and motivated by my eternal truth and present power.

Karmic compensation can also be a source of present-day money experiences, both good and bad. A client once came to me to find out why he hated work so much. He actually didn't mind the activities of his job as much as having to work at all. He made good money, got several weeks of vacation every year, and enjoyed a relatively calm office environment; yet year after year he found himself resenting that part of his life more and more.

Of course it's natural for people *not* to want to spend 40 hours a week working, but this man's reaction was extreme. When he did a past-life regression, he found out why. In a previous incarnation, he'd been a wealthy man, a gentleman of leisure who spent most of his time socializing and playing the *bon vivant.* In that life, he'd gone through all of his money (and a lot of women) without much care or humanitarian considerations. In the later years of that life, he had many regrets—one was that he'd blown his whole fortune, and another was that he'd spent that life being selfish and unaware. These realizations caused him to want to do things differently the next time around—to experience the world in a new way.

His spirit's first intention was to learn to have more appreciation for everything, including money, and to understand its value and not be so cavalier about it. The encoded conclusion was that if he had to work for it, he would appreciate it more. In addition, this life brought him the opportunity to be productive, to work and see the value in that as well. His initial resentment had merely been a lingering longing for his unrestrained past life, but he now knew that wasn't where his soul wanted to go. He redefined his job and found more ways to create joy in the experience. He became more grateful for the money that his work brought him, and he appreciated himself much more because he saw the value that being a productive and responsible individual could bring to his life.

Understanding his past entirely shifted his view of his present. He felt like a different person and moved through his life with a sense of peace unlike any he'd felt before. He looked at the people and things around him with profound appreciation. He'd achieved what his soul longed to do.

3. Karmic "Retribution"

The concept of retribution is one of the most difficult parts of karma to understand. This is the karmic pattern that looks like punishment, but isn't. Like compensation, retribution is a reversal of energy, but it's designed to enlighten the person by allowing him to experience the same kind of energy that he put out in a previous life. For example, if you were critical in a past life, you might come to this Earth plane to experience a relationship where you receive criticism. This allows you to know what that kind of treatment feels like, offering the opportunity to move to a higher intention and become more kind and loving.

Unfortunately, however, this encoded intention may actually dig you deeper into a negative pattern. Let's say you'd been in a marriage where you were abused in a past life. You may have experienced such hurt and rage over that treatment that you encoded hostility and the desire for revenge in your intentions for a future life. It would then be entirely possible for you to come back in a relationship with the same person, this time with you as the aggressor and the other person as the victim. You get your revenge, but you definitely don't move forward.

This kind of back-and-forth role reversal is actually quite common in marriages and parent/child relationships. The process can be so emotionally charged that it can go on and on for many lifetimes—or at least until one of the parties finally decides to pursue the path of genuine honoring and love, choosing to move on to a higher life condition.

SOULUTION

You don't have to go back and relive a role reversal in order to pay anyone back. All you have to do is create the intention to release it. Instead of being passive—or aggressive—remember to live in your authentic power and know that you deserve your own self-care. Bless the experience and the knowledge you've gained from it, and move on to the intention to honor yourself and your process.

Your relationships are brought to you for a purpose. When you think of a problem person, send them your spirit's love and gentle healing light. Affirm: I let go of the past. I see and honor my own eternal worth. In every relationship, I speak my truth and take action on my own behalf, honoring myself and others. I am free to create a new and healthy relationship with myself and everyone around me.

The study of karma can be so interesting, and it can be extremely helpful to know how past events are influencing your present relationships and situations. You could do regressions and learn all sorts of fascinating information about your past—but you can find out about your lessons *right now.* All you have to do is notice the patterns in your present life. Notice the places where you lose your power or try to gain it falsely through hostility, manipulation, or escapism. Ask yourself: *What is my spirit trying to teach me about this? What am I supposed to shift?* Write the answers in your journal.

The lessons of spirit are usually about genuine priorities, self-love, and compassion, as well as finding peace and authentic power in your own life and helping create it for others. Whatever your present pattern or difficulty may be, your soul's desire is always to move toward authenticity and truth. These are rare commodities in our society. Whether it's love, power, or value, the soul's intention is never fraudulent, never superficial, never faulty. And your experience here is to remind you of that.

So no matter what's going on in your life, you can investigate what's blocking you and figure out how to move forward. Ask yourself:

- *What can I do to bring authenticity to my thoughts and behaviors in this situation?*

- *What is the spiritual truth within this experience?*

- *What choices can I make to honor my truth and my value now?*

Meditate on the situation and open yourself to spirit's answers. Keep a notebook close by so that you can jot down any answers you receive. It's also wise to keep a notebook by your bed. Oftentimes your spirit will guide you in your dreams. In fact, you may be surprised by the many ways in which you get the answers you're looking for. Since your spirit backs your honoring choices, it will always help guide you there.

Soul Choices and Shared Karma

In addition to choosing your lessons, your soul also selects another influential factor in your destiny creation, and that's the environment you're born into. Your environment, your family, your location of birth, and where you live—all of these things are a part of your soul's process, and often a part of your karma, too. It's what you do with these elements that determines how you evolve both personally and spiritually.

While all the variables of environment will definitely influence your destiny, they don't have to be the determining factor of your future results. Of course, it's not likely that you'll become a member of the Bolshoi Ballet if you're born into a family of rice farmers in a remote Chinese province—not likely, but in this ever-shrinking world, not impossible either. Your soul gave you the family and environment you have for a reason. Sometimes that reason is to work within it; other times that reason is to break free from it. Instead of being defined by your environment, your spirit and your choice to live your truth can move you forward.

There are many cases of people who've had great success in life in spite of difficult histories and horrible environments. Author and inspirational speaker Dr. Wayne W. Dyer spent much of his youth living in orphanages and foster homes because his father was absent and his mother was extremely poor, yet he has gone on to write numerous books and inspire millions of people around the world. Oprah Winfrey was born into an impoverished family in the South, but she didn't allow that environment to define her either. She, too, has inspired millions; and her soul's intention to take a higher path has created dramatic and positive changes in the lives of individuals, families, and entire communities. The loving energy of both of these people—and many others, including you and me—feeds the Law of Expanding Influence, spreading higher consciousness in accelerated proportions.

Our connection with others is indisputable. We're intrinsically tied to every other being on the planet—and intimately connected to our family and friends. Past-life ties bring us back in search of love and completion, and our soul will strive for peaceful resolution until it's achieved.

Shared karma—along with the lessons it brings—is one of the explanations for the seemingly inexplicable difficulties that can occur within relationships. If a child is sick, it may be that the souls of all the members of that family have the intention to work on something together. Perhaps a past life had shifted their priorities or led them away from their faith. This experience may cause them to learn to trust in a higher power and reprioritize what they find meaningful. Or maybe their shared intention is to renew an understanding of the eternal nature of life. Certainly, at the heart of this experience—and most others—there is a lesson of enduring love and trust, an awareness that the soul lives on and brings its light and clarity to all. Embracing this truth creates profound equanimity, a valuable life lesson that can enrich us all.

Whatever you experience, your choice to live in trust and love spreads those qualities in the lives of those around you. All you have to do is follow your spirit's path. Your soul's intention is a beautiful thing, although it may sometimes take you to unlikely (and seemingly unwanted) places. Look for the meaning hidden in each experience. In it you may find the door to heaven itself.

Cycles of Learning

Oftentimes your karmic lessons may be embedded in a primary issue, expanding your spirit's intention to a much broader scope. Like most of us, you may have a *life lesson* that your soul is driving you to experience and understand. This may lead you in a vastly different direction from your personal drive for prosperity. You may have the desire to win the lottery, but your soul may want you to learn self love. In terms of the eternal perspective, which do you think is more important—and more enriching?

Whether or not it feels prosperous, your spirit's intention will always take you to far, far greater wealth. Open your heart to this truth, because whatever lesson your soul may have in mind, if you're *not* willing to work on it, you can rest assured that it will keep reappearing in your life.

In fact, the *life lesson* is one of the biggest reasons why you keep experiencing the same issues over and over again. It's profoundly important, a high priority in your eternal process.

Some of the most common life lessons are:

- Self-love
- Speaking your truth
- Finding a higher meaning and purpose
- Releasing attachment or addiction
- Reverence
- Equanimity and self-mastery
- Divine expression
- Authentic empowerment
- Living with integrity
- Compassion and expanding unity

Many times our lessons are about personal growth, which often means not wallowing in the immediate gratification of the ego's desires. It can also call for us to transcend our doubts and fears and move into trust and abiding faith, no matter what circumstances we may face. These and all life lessons are big attraction factors. In your heart and soul, the lesson comes first. And when you move into that lofty resolution, you'll find that your genuine desires have more power there.

So if you see any of the above issues repeating for you, it could be the very purpose of your life to resolve and master them. But healing these issues isn't your spirit's only motivation, and your lesson doesn't belong to you alone. Sometimes you come to this life to teach and share what you've learned. Teaching, sharing, and giving are all part of the spirit's shared consciousness of love.

Spirit gets great joy out of doing for others—so much so that there may be times in your life—or even entire lifetimes—where you find yourself in a cycle of loving service. This may call for great effort, but that doesn't diminish the joy at all. And if you immerse yourself in this joy of service, it's the very act of giving that allows you to receive. Like an exhausted parent who's putting a toy together in the middle of the night on Christmas Eve, the blessing of seeing the gift received is well worth the energy.

In fact, sharing yourself doesn't have to be difficult at all. You'll find that when you've learned your life lesson, you're so empowered and excited that you'll want to share your energy in loving service to those around you. The key is balance—mixing genuine motivation with action and self-honoring. Your time and your life energy are valuable to you, and they're truly valuable to the world at large. The service you bring to yourself and others is a gift that expands exponentially.

All of the seasons of your life—both personal and eternal—are bountiful opportunities. The light of your spirit's intention will lead you through many cycles of giving and receiving, learning and growing, striving and enjoying.

Love is the big lesson, the greatest service, and the finest gift. When you bring love to your consciousness, even for just a moment, your eternal soul smiles. And that gratitude expands, sending waves of cascading appreciation, touching the hearts of distant, unknown souls—brothers and sisters on their own journey of truth. In that moment, your achievement is great, although nothing external seems to have changed. Don't be fooled, however. Sharing love is the pinnacle of soul desire; and as such, it's the source of your deepest, most profoundly attractive vibration.

CHAPTER NINE

MASTERING THE MYSTERIES

"In every human being there is a special heaven whole and unbroken."

— PARACELSUS

As you look more deeply at the various influences that contribute to your life, it becomes apparent that there are certainly a lot of factors being thrown into the mix. You might think that there are too many layers to work on, but it's precisely because there's so much to deal with that you have to be willing to be more conscious—and more conscientious—in responding to everything that happens to you.

After all, a lot of things may influence your health, but that doesn't mean you should take no responsibility for it yourself. Yes, environment and heredity could be contributing factors, but you could significantly influence your well-being yourself by taking control of the physical elements of your daily life, such as exercising, eating well, and getting plenty of rest. Would it make sense to say that since you can't control every part of your physical destiny, you're not going to bother working on it at all?

Well, your personal destiny is the same way. You could just say, "What's the use?" but then your lack of consciousness and purposeful direction would simply drag you deeper into the problems you already have. Instead, you can take action in your daily life, work on healing the issues and reversing the patterns, and keep moving forward in the direction of your dreams.

You always have the option to use the power of your consciousness to change any adverse situation and create a different direction. Within this power is the ability to move through the difficult cycles and find value and enlightenment on the other side. In fact, you can bring this enlightened view and inner power to any step in the process. There are ways to get through any cycle, but before we look at those steps, there's one more important force that has yet to be explored.

On the Seesaw with Yin and Yang

The ancient symbol of yin and yang is a very powerful metaphor for me. In fact, I used it on the cover of a recent book as an icon of adjacent possibilities—that is, a symbol to remind us of the many options that we face in every moment. But the force of yin and yang is more than a metaphor; it's an actual energy current that moves through the Universe. These are also cycles in the flow of nature and in the process of humankind that represent movement from passive to active and back to passive again.

There are times that are meant to be yielding and receptive, where great change happens under the surface while things seem quiet above. These are the cycles of yin. In these periods, you're often called upon to rethink your regular activity. You may be accustomed to aggressive action, which is a typical yang energy, but if you find yourself within the yin, it may be time to let that go and find an approach that's more harmonic with the more subtle energy going on in your life.

You can tell you're in a yin cycle if you're feeling shut down, passive, and even stuck in forced inactivity. Yin is a time of quiet, but it's also a time of radical intuition, gestation, and gathering energies in. As a result, it can also be a time of great receptivity. If you're in a yin cycle, you need to know that. You would never plant the seeds of beautiful flowers in the frozen fields of December and expect them to blossom in the spring. That would be fighting the forces of nature instead of working with the energy cycle you're in. Sometimes your life, your spirit, or the Universe demands that you stop and regroup before you go on.

There's an old adage that says: "When the seas are stormy, the fisherman stays home and repairs the nets." But this doesn't just apply to fishing! When your seas are stormy, there may be something you need to repair. Go within; investigate what's truly going on. Take time to regroup and reflect. Follow all the steps for cycling through—don't just settle for muddling through a time of reflection and inner change.

Sometimes you may be faced with demands of the opposite kind, finding yourself taking action upon action in an ongoing creative pursuit. These are periods of yang energy. Yang times are logical and even forceful periods of outgoing energy, activity, and creativity. They often initiate new beginnings and great outer change. Depending on your own energy, a yang cycle could push you into activity. For instance, a sailor on a stormy sea wouldn't just go below and repair the nets. He'd have to hurry to trim the sails and maintain control of the rudder. The environment in both these examples is the same, but requires two different responses depending on the individual's purpose in the situation.

This is true in the modern world as well. Many people would call recent economic times a strong example of yin energy, and I have to agree. As a society, we need to reflect on our past patterns and rework our approaches to money. These times of quiet gathering are indicating the inner change that we as a group consciousness must make.

Yet there are individuals within this time who are definitely in a yang reaction. They're buying up foreclosed homes, expanding development, and even starting new businesses. You need to identify your own energy cycle. If you're in a group consciousness, you don't have to follow it unthinkingly. It would, however, be helpful to understand its momentum in your life and then make decisions based on your own personal energy stages. This is why identifying the cycle you're in is the first important step in moving on.

Stepping Through the Cycles

There are certain things that you can do to maximize all of your experiences. The most important thing is to bring your consciousness to them. If you move through your life unconsciously, you lose numerous opportunities for self-empowerment and enrichment. However, if you become conscious about what you're going through and why, you can make informed decisions that will bring you a far greater sense of gratification and personal control.

In fact, this is often the reason you're faced with the inner and outer challenges in your life. Dr. Darren Weissman calls them "symptoms," indications that something needs to be taken care of deep within the subconscious mind. This is significant, so let's have a look at the steps you can take to arrive at a greater awareness and stronger sense of purpose and power, no matter what cycle you may be in.

Step 1: Identify the Cycle

Sometimes there isn't a lot that you can do externally to hurry a cycle along, yet if you want to heal or transform the cyclical energy you're in, it's helpful to identify it first. Are you in a cycle of loss—a period of transition from ending to beginning? If so, it will be important to identify that change for yourself. Perhaps you're in a time of shifting—a personal or professional change. Or perhaps a new cycle has already begun for you, and you're in a time of growth and expansion. Whatever passage you may be going through, it's important to name it and claim it so that you can move on. Even if you feel you're in a cycle of perpetuation, maintenance of the status quo where nothing seems to be changing at all, you still have the opportunity to use it as a time of growth and shifting consciousness.

Identifying your present cycle is important for four reasons:

1. You can more easily align yourself with these natural energies, creating a greater synchronicity and flow.

2. Understanding where you are allows you to release resistance—which can bring you comfort, receptivity, and greater peace of mind.

3. Identifying your cycle will bring about a deeper understanding of your own personal purpose, as well as the meaning of the experience in your life.

4. On both a spiritual and personal level, knowing your cycle gives you the wisdom necessary to move your entire life forward and help you break through to the next cycle of experience.

This step of identification is an important one, as a client named Gigi recently realized. She'd always had problems with hostile and competitive people at work, so she'd changed jobs frequently, only to find similar situations with her new co-workers. She was once again thinking of changing, but she was having difficulty finding a new position.

Since she had trouble finding a transfer this time around, I suggested she might be in a yin cycle, and it could be a good time to reflect on all the problems she'd been having. After investigating several incidents, we realized that she'd been reacting passive-aggressively, letting people walk all over her until she got so fed up that she finally exploded.

She implemented some new behaviors; she became more assertive and started speaking her truth right from the beginning. This was difficult for Gigi at first—she only had experience in her two polar reactions—silent submission and emotional self-defense. With courage and practice, however, she was able to speak up at appropriate times and express herself clearly, firmly, and unemotionally. As a result, her co-workers became more respectful, and she developed a far greater sense of control and self-actualization.

Gigi no longer feels the need to escape, but she realized that part of her frustration stemmed from the desire for more stimulating work. She still plans to transfer, but in the meantime, she's enjoying her job more and is changing the very way she interacts with others—the way she's responded her entire life. And as a result of this profound inner change, when she does move on, she'll attract a different type of environment with people who respect her. It had felt as though Gigi was stuck, but it was really a cycle of major transformation; and if she hadn't identified that, she couldn't have taken the necessary steps to discover the honoring, strong, and self-directed person she was capable of being.

Step 2: Open Your Heart to Spirit's Assistance and Guidance

There is a wealth of power and information available to you at all times. Where you see obstruction, your spirit sees growth. Where you see difficulty, your spirit sees opportunity. So when you take the time to perceive the situation from your eternal perspective, you'll get an entirely different point of view. Instead of panicking or taking things personally, this spiritual perspective will help you arrive at a more peaceful understanding. And instead of becoming a victim, awakening to your spiritual intention will bring you all the power you need to turn things around.

So meditate, and ask your soul to reveal the deeper purpose in your present experience. Whether the situation is good or bad, there's higher meaning there. Open your mind and heart to receiving the guidance that comes. You'll be amazed by the inspiration and peace this brings. In fact, this connection with your Source and Higher Power is one of the greatest gifts that investigating the experience can offer.

Sometimes the power you find is exactly what you need to see things through. Such was the case for a friend of mine who found herself in a time of forced transformation. She'd developed an alcohol addiction; and as is the case with so many, she finally reached the point where she must give it up or lose it all—her boyfriend, her job, and even her friends. She opened to spirit, receiving guidance, strength, and discipline. It was very difficult for her, but she was able to gain control over her addiction. She swears she couldn't have done it without the guidance and power that spirit brought her.

In addition to asking for guidance, though, also remember to direct your intentions to a higher vibration and a personal goal. Announce to the spirit world, to the Universe, and to yourself that you're ready to receive something better and brighter. Your willingness to honor and move past any difficulty may actually accelerate things and clear the way. Always know that you'll move forward more easily because you've connected with the everlasting and inestimable power within.

So whatever you face, never forget this truth: *It's within that peaceful, nonstriving place in your eternal life—your soul—where your greatest power lies.* Even if all else fails you, your choice to live in that peaceful, powerful place will always see you through. Don't dismiss the step of opening to your spirit's peace and power. It's part of the bigger truth, the directing force that so many people forget when working with the laws of attraction.

Step 3: Honor the Feelings of the Experience

Most people never think about how they *want* to experience the emotions of their cycles. They tend to just react without any consciousness of their emotional options. In good times, of course, they experience happiness. In difficult times, they react with sadness, anger, and grief.

But emotional cycling is as much a part of the process as the experience itself. If there's a loss—whether it's the end of a relationship or the loss of a job—you must honor the grief and vent the feelings that go with it. You may, however, be hesitant to get into the emotion—either because it's too painful or because you feel it's too negative. But remember the truth about attraction that we discussed earlier: unexpressed grief stays in your personal energy field; and even if you ignore it, the subtle yet pervasive resonance continues to vibrate with agitation and sadness.

If, on the other hand, you express it, you will get that energy out of your life-force vibration. Talking, writing, or crying about your honest feelings will get the darkness out of your consciousness so that you can heal and move on to those better and brighter results. In fact, when you honor and vent your feelings about the experience, it can not only change what you're going through, it can change your whole life—allowing you to see more clearly, feel more authentically, and act in ways that are far healthier for you.

Whatever your feelings may be, you can get them out without losing power over them. If you find yourself falling into a victim mentality, make the choice to take your power back. Continue to vent the hurt or anger, but then acknowledge that although you have those emotions, you are not defined by them.

Affirm the following:

- *It is safe for me to feel deeply. I know this is a part of my process, and I am strong and resilient.*

- *I express my feelings honestly and appropriately, and I hold my own self-love in my heart.*

- *No matter how I may feel now, I know that I have within me the power to heal and create a happy life.*

Step 4: Find the Real Meaning in the Situation and Identify the Changes Required

No matter what you go through—good or bad—there's always a gift, a lesson, or an opportunity in every experience. The real worth in any situation comes from finding the true meaning and purpose behind it—then making the changes that are required.

Unfortunately, most of us get so caught up in the drama that we skip this part of the process entirely. A man gets passed over for a promotion; and he spends weeks, months, or even years going to work with feelings of resentment and betrayal. A woman gets dumped in a romantic relationship; and she makes the conclusion that no man can be trusted, spending her days in hopelessness and longing.

These are natural emotional reactions and should be expressed, but they should *not* be embraced as a way of life. They simply don't represent the truth in the situation—the true meaning, the lesson involved, or the honest interpretation. Nor does this type of reaction encourage the changes necessary for healing, happiness, and higher vibration.

To merely stew in bitterness misses some of the most important opportunities of life. People think their opportunities come in the offer of a new job or the introduction of a new person, but these pale in comparison to the importance of our opportunities for personal growth and deep understanding.

Every transition is a cycle of learning—whether you choose to take advantage of it or not. In every single hardship and every moment of joy, there's a fundamental purpose of higher awareness or personal growth. The lessons in life are many, and they usually point right back to your view of yourself and the world around you.

A big question in many lessons is: *Are you going to love, accept, and honor yourself no matter what is going on?* Until the answer to this is *yes,* you will keep experiencing situations where your self-regard is challenged by a lack of regard from others and the world. Your lessons of self-love and self-priority require you to not only treat yourself well, but also to expect to be treated well by others. This is true in any relationship, whether it's romantic, platonic, or even professional. Your choice to honor and respect yourself must be a firm intention within, and it must also extend to the outside world. You deserve to be treated civilly and with respect in any relationship; and when you create this treatment within yourself and request it from others, a major life lesson will be learned. This will cause a shift in consciousness so significant that it will manifest in amazingly wonderful ways throughout your life.

The choice of self-love and self-honoring is a huge piece of the attraction puzzle, but it's just one of the many opportunities for learning in any experience. There are *personal* lessons like communication and self-discipline. There are *spiritual* lessons such as faith, trust, and eternal resilience. There are even *tactical* lessons, important changes of a logistical nature that could make all the difference.

Tactical changes can be some of the easiest, yet even these can be overlooked. A client once came to see me about following his dream of making music. He composed, sang, and played guitar and piano beautifully. What was standing in his way, however, was his location. He lived in a small town in central Ohio—not really conducive to establishing a musical career. Although he had gotten some gigs in some pubs in the area, he knew that would be the extent of it if he didn't move to an environment that would afford him more opportunities. This was a tactical change, and it meant pulling up roots, but his family was willing to help make his dreams come true.

Some lessons combine all the issues—tactical, personal, and spiritual. Your willingness to look deeply into the situation to find out what's really going on—and what you need to do about it—is one of the most powerful choices you can make, and it can change your life entirely. This is what becoming conscious is all about! So don't be blind to the real issues, and don't be distracted by your ego's interpretation of things.

The Titanic wasn't sunk by the tip of the iceberg; it was sunk by the huge obstacle hidden below the quiet sea. Your own energy obstacles are like that. A situation may seem like no big deal—and it may seem easier to just ignore it and keep on responding in the same old ways. But keep in mind that if you take this approach, your dreams could be sunk by what's going on underneath your awareness.

This is where your true power lies—bringing your consciousness to all the experiences of your life. The ability to make changes can only come from introspection and examination. Without these, you're at the mercy of old habits and energy patterns. But when you start to investigate the true purpose of a situation, you'll find the lesson within. You can then choose to move into it, clear it, and move on to better things—or you can bypass it and repeat the experience later.

Step 5: Determine the Direction You Want to Go Next—and Start Taking Action

Learning a lesson may require you to make different decisions, such as letting go of something that's just not working and establishing something entirely new. It may be creating a habit that you've never engaged in before; it may be constructing a new belief system filled with healthy and optimistic conclusions. You may need to take steps toward healing or redefinition. Whatever it is, let yourself be open to the *action* needed.

Sometimes the ideas for the new action will come through networking with people of like mind. Sometimes the action is internal and introspective; yet at other points, the action may be external and practical.

To find out what the action is, you need to ask yourself two important questions:

1. *What do I want to achieve—in the present and in the future?* (This includes *inner* achievement.)

2. *What do I need to do (differently) to achieve it?*

Now you may be thinking that you've already been working on what you want to achieve, but if you're in a cycle of transformation or obstruction, there may be something else you're supposed to be doing. This is what cycling in and cycling out is all about; you must see the cycle you're in as part of the message about where to go next.

Even if the action is only internal, such as shifting consciousness and drawing new conclusions, it's still significant work in the energetic realm. Achievement happens on many levels, although it may not be readily apparent to the outside world. Most people consider monetary success and acquisition to be the major signs of accomplishment these days, but real achievements come in the many little victories of the heart, mind, and soul. So let yourself take these kinds of actions first, and you'll be surprised by the amazing inspiration you get about how to proceed on your external path.

SOULUTION

Identify the cycle you're in and align yourself with the energies there to maximize the power of this time. Open yourself to spirit's guidance and the ever-present power that this unwavering part of your identity can bring about. Search out the true purpose for this experience in your life. Remember this: it's up to you to define your experiences, so do not allow your experiences to define you!

As you develop a clarity of understanding and take the inner action, you'll become more and more prepared for transition and forward motion. You'll develop the confidence, wisdom, and insight to take the external action that's needed. And in time, the internal benefits that this cycle has brought to your life will manifest in truly valuable ways in the physical world.

Divorce Redux

I myself experienced the difference that bringing one's consciousness and intention to a difficult time can make. I had to go through this process of cycling when each of my first two marriages ended. During my first divorce I acted unconsciously. I allowed myself to go through the whole thing being numb and unaware. I expressed very little anger or grief, although under the surface those feelings ran deep. I had no intentions about where I wanted to go next, only the knowledge that my marriage was ending. It's hard to believe now, but at the time I didn't even give any thought to my thinking!

This was a big mistake. That marriage had been difficult for me, and I was engaged in some pretty negative thoughts about men and relationships. However, I did nothing except try to get through the experience. I muddled through, got out on my own, and started dating again. I had no consciousness of my opportunities for change, no clarity about what had gone wrong or what this experience was supposed to bring to my life—and no awareness that I even had the option to set new intentions for the future. But as a result of my unaware attitude and emotionally unconscious reaction, I was given the opportunity to do the whole thing all over again during my second divorce.

This time I decided to do everything differently. I kept a notebook by my bed, and every time I got angry or sad, I wrote those feelings down. I wrote them in the form of a letter to my ex-husband—not to send, just to vent—which I did every single time an emotion (positive or negative) came up. I found that I was experiencing all sorts of feelings: longing for the relationship to continue, relief that it had ended, anger at my ex, and gratitude as well. Such conflicting emotions are all a natural part of the grief cycle, and by writing them down I was eventually able to come to a place of balance and control.

I also did some writing to identify and reverse the negative conclusions about my worth, my world, and my future. I originally had thoughts such as: *There are no good guys out there; it's impossible to find a happy and healthy relationship.* But through my writings, I was able to identify and change those toxic conclusions. I wrote down new thoughts, such as: *I'm worthy of a great relationship; there are wonderful guys out there. I have a great future whether I'm in a relationship or not.* I meditated on the truth of these statements—and on my own deserving—and that really cemented those intentions for me.

I also created a plan for self-reliance. I'd found out through both of those experiences that I was too dependent on men, and I wanted to be more autonomous. So I created a plan with the specific steps I needed to take to become more resourceful and self-actualized. I also created other new intentions for my future. I intended to establish a happy life for myself, independent of a man. I also planned to do more of the things I loved, like skiing and white-water rafting, which I had given up when I was in my previous relationships.

Most important, I decided to "do" my next relationship differently: I vowed to speak my truth, to honor myself, and to make reasonable requests for respectful and kind treatment. I was so determined about this that I knew I'd never accept anything less ever again. And although I didn't really have any desire to get married again, I made a list of the kinds of qualities I wanted in the next man I dated. I included things such as *available, respectful, communicative, fun loving,* and *stable.* It turns out, that's exactly what I got!

Spirit actually assisted me with that. Through my meditations at the time, I was inspired by a wonderful visualization that has now become the "Attracting Love" track on my *Act to Attract* CD. In it, I visualized a hologram of my higher self sending out waves of the qualities I desired. I knew they were moving into the energetic realm, and I supported that intention by consciously engaging in those qualities in my daily life. In addition to the actions I was taking internally and externally, I used that holographic visualization every night. Amazingly, I met my current husband within four months.

This experience was utterly illuminating and life changing for me. I'd gone through two similar cycles of divorce, but I approached them entirely differently. It's no surprise that I attracted very different results. I'm now with someone who is stable, reliable, loving, fun, and very funny—all because I dealt with that cycle instead of just muddling through it.

You can do the same! No matter what cycle you're in, let it be a time of real transformation for you. Identify what you're going through, vent the emotions, and honor the process. Create a plan, set your intentions, and remember to support those intentions in the choices and thoughts of your daily life.

Your consciousness has the power to thwart adversity, but if you remain unconscious in your difficult times, you'll simply give that power away. Instead, you can choose to embrace the experience, all the while letting go of the ego and the outcomes. Do the inner work and see where your eternal path will lead. Live in the consciousness of love and trust and you'll find that your difficult cycles can turn into magical new beginnings.

PART III

TRUTH or CONSEQUENCES

"Each day, each hour, every instant, I am choosing what I want to look upon, the sounds I want to hear, the witnesses to what I want to be the truth for me."

— A COURSE IN MIRACLES

CHAPTER TEN

THE LIES PEOPLE LIVE

"Lay bare the bones of your feelings, expose them no matter the pain or suffering or humility involved. For only when your hurts and griefs and torments and fears have been cast away can you find your true being and see the nature of the power that flows forever through the depths of your soul."

— U. S. ANDERSEN

Once you're aware of the various factors that could be influencing your destiny creation, you have all the pieces necessary to put this vast and beautiful puzzle together. It takes some thought to figure out how all the pieces fit, and that means bringing your consciousness to every area of your life.

This is one of the most empowering and liberating things you can do: to become conscious of your higher intentions; to let go of the urgency and striving; and to move through the cycles of your life with grace, peace, and awareness. All of this can be achieved by stepping back and viewing your experiences with a greater understanding of both the meaning and the options hidden within. And underneath it all, there could be one major factor upon which the truth of the whole process is based. It's the most important piece of the puzzle—the one around which all the other pieces fit. It's an issue of identity, and it poses a question of great proportion!

The Big Consciousness Question . . .

Have you been living a lie—even a little one? Don't be too quick to deny it. You may not even realize that your life has been moving in that direction for years. Like the rest of us, you've probably become accustomed to wearing a mask that's been covering a gap in your truth. It could be a deep gash—one that goes down to your very soul.

Two important falsehoods need to be set right in order to heal the distance between your eternal soul and your personality. As you discovered in Chapter 6, the gap between the soul's intentions and the ego's desires is a significant tear in the truth that must be dealt with. But an equally compelling force is the split between the profound identity of your spirit and your present self-definition.

Once we become embroiled in the dramas of this earthly experience, a great difference forms between how we see ourselves and what we remember of our spirit's true identity. This fundamental break creates a huge dilemma in the human experience. Somewhere deep within our unspoken memory, we know that our soul defines us as eternal and powerful, light-beings of inestimable value, inextricably connected to the Source of love and of all creativity.

On the other side of the experience, most of us don't even think of how we define ourselves. But if we were to give it some thought, we'd probably view ourselves according to our human limitations—the focus of which is driven by our history and the ongoing roles we continue to play. Depending on our specific childhood dramas, we're likely to then go through our lives with an undercurrent of confusion, longing, or discontent. We try to compensate for what we feel is missing, and we constantly strive to fix what we find faulty within ourselves and our lives.

But this undercurrent of self-deceit spins a false life force that can only set you up for chronic disappointment. The lies that you live will ultimately betray you and actually become the source of far more obstacles than achievements. As a result, *the most important truth that you have to investigate is your own!* After all, it's very hard to align with the authentic energies of the Universe when you're unknowingly living—and projecting—a lie.

Remember this fundamental truth about attraction: *The Universe responds to your whole life force, not just your surface intentions.* This is one of the key ingredients that many people miss when they're trying to create a different destiny. What you may not realize, however, is that it's very difficult to create a new and improved future when you keep projecting a consciousness based in the same old false beliefs of the past.

Your life force—your daily energy and consciousness creation—is the generator of your ongoing happiness (or lack thereof). As such, it represents you in the Universe and is at the heart of what you attract and manifest. Although the other factors discussed in the previous section also influence destiny creation, making a consistent and conscious effort to shift your life-force energy is the most powerful thing you can do to change both the quality of your life now and your results in the future.

SOULUTION

The most important requirement of consciousness created reality isn't fulfilled by focusing on what you want. In order to change what you experience in this life, you must clear your perceptions of the unhealthy views and habits of your history and awaken yourself to the power of your truth.

The big question is: Do you want to keep reliving the past—or do you want to use the present to create a new truth and a new future? This is one of the noblest and most beneficial choices that you can make. When you consciously choose your own self-definition, you completely change the essence of all that you experience and attract.

Debby's Story

Ever since she was very young, Debby was taught that it absolutely mattered what people thought of her. Her parents impressed upon her that this should be her primary concern. She was told that she must learn to be perfect in every way, and she embraced this lie with utter ferocity.

Throughout her life, Debby based everything she did on this need to be perfect and impress people. She always made sure her house was spotless. She threw perfect parties with magnificent centerpieces and sparkling stemware. The kids always had the best labels on their clothes, and Debby made sure she always drove new cars—whether she could afford them or not.

Debby was so successful at living this lie of perfectionism that her life *appeared* impeccable in every way. But the relentless striving and worrying about what people thought took its toll. In her mid-20s, she started to experience anxiety, which slowly turned into panic-attack syndrome. Not only did she feel the stress of having to be perfect, now she had to be perfect while she was having panic attacks!

Surprisingly, Debby muddled through this misery for nearly two decades. She lived a life of hell, having panic attacks every single day, yet never giving up the pretense and the extraordinary effort of presenting a wonderful life. The physical symptoms of this ongoing stress finally became too much to bear.

Amazingly, it wasn't until she came in for treatment for her anxiety that she found out she'd been living a lie. Although she was in her mid-40s, it had never even once occurred to her that it didn't matter what people thought—or that trying to be perfect was a huge source of stress in addition to being a waste of time. Upon closer investigation, however, it became clear to her that unless she eliminated this pattern, she'd never be able to release her anxiety.

Yet this had been Debby's story, and she'd lived it with gusto. Seeking perfection had become her purpose, and pretending to achieve it had become her self-definition. So when she was faced with letting all that go, she felt some strong resistence. After all, it's hard to find out you've been living a lie.

Over time, however, Debby saw that it greatly reduced her stress when she stopped worrying about impressing people. She taught herself that it was both safe and healthy to be imperfect. She let go of the striving, and for the very first time she lived her life the way she wanted—not the way she thought others expected. She realized that in perpetuating her ongoing lie of perfection, she'd never, ever been able to just relax. But when she stopped acting from fear and started making choices out of loving self-acceptance, her panic and anxiety completely disappeared.

Debby could easily see the life lesson her lie had created. She used the technique called *cognitive restructuring* (described later in this chapter) to let go of all the old demands, and she went on to establish a new truth where peace was more important than striving, and genuine happiness was far more important than perfectionism.

> **Debby's lie:** *I need to be perfect and have a perfect life. I need to impress people to gain their approval.*
>
> **Debby's truth:** *I am valuable just as I am. In truth, my soul and my life are perfect right now. I deserve to approve of myself without conditions or striving. I can let go of the struggle and live in peace.*

Opening to the truth that she deserved her own self-love completely set Debby free to be herself and live authentically. And—as it always does—love's expanding influence moved out into the lives and hearts of her whole family. Debby was anxiety free, and everyone was more relaxed and far more comfortable living in their wonderfully imperfect state. In addition, her kids received something they needed much more than designer clothes: the presence of a peaceful, loving mom and freedom from perpetuating the immobilizing lie of perfectionism in their lives.

Identifying Your Story

Everybody has a story—everybody! Depending on what your history is and how much you allow it to define you, it can be powerful enough to influence your reality, including what you attract. You probably don't realize it, but if you're like most of us, you're actually living in a play that was created by someone else. You may be the main character, but the lines you speak and the actions you take were scripted for you long ago. As long as you remain unconscious of your option to change that script, you're likely to be at the mercy of external events rather than the master of them.

You may have never thought about it before, but we all live according to the unspoken assumptions of our self-definition. These are identity markers about both our character and nature, and although we may not be aware of them, they form the very fabric of our life force. These encoded characteristics are so powerful that they have the ability to direct the course of our destiny, even influencing the cycles we find ourselves in and influencing our reactions to them.

If you want to change what you've been attracting, you need to ask yourself this important question: *Are you living any old lies—or are you driven by your most empowering truth?* To find out the details, use your journal to answer the questions below. As you do so, you'll begin to identify the patterns in your life that form your consciousness. Think about your responses in terms of your most prominent emotions and most deeply held beliefs.

1. How would you define (not describe) yourself?
2. What emotions do you tend to live in most? (Could they be, for example, fear, worry, trust, peace, happiness, or sadness?)
3. What is your nature? (Do you tend to be passive, aggressive, thorough, or indifferent?)
4. How do you talk to yourself? (Are you demanding, loving, encouraging, or critical?)
5. How do you talk to others? (Are you judgmental, complimentary, assertive, or submissive?)
6. What do you prioritize in your life? (List the top four items that you devote most of your time to.)
7. What do you think of yourself—honestly?
8. What is your story? How were you treated, talked to, and prioritized?

9. What were you taught to believe about yourself and the world?

10. How are these beliefs affecting you today?

It may take some time and honest self-investigation, but doing this exercise is well worth it. The answers to the questions reveal the truth about your present consciousness, as well as the source of any problems from the past. Whether those answers are positive or negative will also indicate the kinds of results you're likely to attract. Your life force reaches out to create consequences for you and for the world; and it's largely controlled by your patterns of belief, action, and reaction. So if you're wondering why the same problems keep sprouting up over and over again, it's because you keep sticking to your old story—holding on to the mental and emotional habits that were formed there.

You may believe that those habits are inextricably yours, something you're destined to maintain no matter what. But it's time to sort out the lies of the past and understand that your old story is just somebody else's myth. It's time to finally realize that you *do* have the power to let go of the habits and hindrances of past beliefs. When you release the misinformation, you move on to living a clear and empowered truth. In fact, if your history diminishes you or skews your truth in any way, it's an absolute *must* that you vent the emotions, let go of false conclusions, redefine yourself, and reclaim your power now.

⚖

Split Definitions

The most important reason for understanding your old story is so you can identify and release the lies that may have been embedded within it. In living out the roles, expectations, and misinformation that others have given you, you may have unwittingly embraced some very disempowering choices that have become energy blocks, holding you back from realizing both your truth and your potential to reach your goals. If you want to move your life in a different direction, it will be necessary to heal your wounded consciousness and set up a new system of more honest and empowering beliefs and behaviors.

Again, a big part of the problem is based in the schism between spiritual definition and personal experience. Living in the falsehoods perpetuated by your history draws you farther and farther away from the realization of the guiding influence of your spirit's peace, presence, and power. This very disquieting disconnect also invokes an intrinsic truth about attraction that can't be avoided: *The core of your ability to be happy is largely built upon your self-definition.* When your whole life force is based on childhood lies that degrade, dismiss, or disempower you, it will be virtually impossible to create a self-definition that projects a positive, happy consciousness—or even acknowledges your innate power to change things. This denial of spirit not only drains your life force, it expands your sense of being disconnected from the world, making you feel lonely and isolated and drawing you deeper into the lie.

As you can see, this is far too big an issue to ignore. The old, false stories—no matter how deeply ingrained—have to be left behind. Any lies must be rewritten, and your heart and mind must open to your truth. Reconciling your soul's intention and definition is an alignment that will completely turn your life around.

Such is the healing power of truth—it changes your life force from the inside out, from the core of your being to all that you know. Whether you realize it or not, it's actually this truth that you've been seeking all along. Through all of your pursuits, in your deepest longings and desires, the inner solution has always been within but has somehow gotten lost in the lies.

Lost in the Lies

Many people have no idea what their truth may be. They've lived so long in the lies of their history that they can't see anything else. Many, in fact, don't have any desire to even face this issue. They're utterly convinced that all solutions come from outside. They also believe that they either can't or shouldn't change who or what they are—even if what they are is toxic to themselves. This is the power of the subconscious mind. It causes us to fight for our history instead of release it. And it compels us to defend our falsehoods with righteous ownership. After all, what should we believe in? Could it be that much of what we've been taught has been a lie? It's not only possible, it's entirely likely; and it's time to identify those lies so that we can finally leave them behind.

A lot of books on attraction advise you to avoid focusing on which you do *not* want. They say that focusing on what you don't want will actually cause you to get more of it. Yet psychologically speaking, this is actually an important step in moving toward getting what you *do* want. You don't have to obsess, but you do have to be prepared for a little self-analysis. If you don't recognize what needs to be changed, there's no way you can do anything different. But if you can identify the hidden patterns that have been causing you problems—whether beliefs, emotions, self-treatment, or what you've been accepting from others—you can integrate the changes necessary to solve them. In fact, a surprising number of people have a difficult time identifying exactly what it is they want, yet they can easily recognize what they don't want.

For example, a woman once brought her husband in for couples therapy. She said she was unhappy, and when I asked her what would make things better, she said she didn't know. However, when I asked her what had made her unhappy, she could easily identify that. She said she didn't want her husband to criticize her so much, and that gave us the opening we needed. I worked with him on breaking that pattern, and then we added what she realized she *did* want, like demonstrations of affection and genuine respect. We were able to change things, but only by identifying and getting rid of what she didn't want first.

The same is true with the lies people live. If you remain impervious to your negative patterns of mental and emotional reactions, it could be very difficult to eradicate the false behaviors and responses that are keeping you and your life force down. But if you can identify what you need to change, it will empower you to release the past and create a higher vibration in your present perception—and a far greater quality of life with respect to the experiences yet to come.

So let's look at some of the most common lies that people live. Identify those that resemble your patterns and history the most. These are important issues that must be resolved. Remember, the Universe won't respond to your surface intentions if they're being used to cover up a life built on the energy of lies.

1. Lies of self-negation and finding yourself faulty: This pattern is revealed in the tendency to judge, demean, or criticize yourself, whether it be limited to specific issues of your life or whether it's a pervasive pattern. This lie is based in a history of being criticized or watching others be criticized. But even if you were told that there were valid reasons for such judgment, you need to know that the information you were given was filtered through someone else's estrangement from their own truth. Included in this pattern is the lie of never being good enough, which you may be perpetuating in your self-view today. You need to remember, however, that no matter how convincing your training was, all of your self-criticism and faultfinding is a false assessment of your true value. So it's time to let it go!

2. Lies of performance, perfectionism, and people pleasing: This is closely related to self-negation, but these unhealthy patterns force you to be something you're not in an ongoing attempt to live up to fraudulent standards placed upon you by a childhood authority, present peers, or society itself. But beware, when you lose your self-acceptance for any reason, you create perpetual striving and fundamental unhappiness that distort both your spiritual truth and your life-force energy. A big part of this deceit is the belief that others have the power to impose their expectations on you—but you don't have to buy into other people's priorities anymore. *As a thinking adult, it's you who places all the demands of your life upon yourself.* Living your truth requires you to set boundaries and live free of false priorities. Let go of the need to perform and seek approval. Know that you're perfect just as you are.

3. Lies of worry, fear, and the need for control: These distortions are built around two main anxieties: fear of the world and its unknowns, and worry that you won't be able to handle what may come up. It can be paralyzing to try to control every variable and ensure that things will always go well. Difficulties may arise, but that's all a part of the cycles of life. Through it all, however, you can believe in yourself and remain optimistic. Believe in your own resourcefulness, and always trust in your ability to deal with things. The greatest control you'll ever have is when you choose to let go and trust.

4. Lies of arrogance, hostility, and false power: If you think you achieve a sense of power or superiority through intimidation, you're fooling yourself! The only thing your judgment is achieving is separation from Universal synchronicity. You also need to realize that your desperate attempts for superiority are really fear-based compensations rooted in the need to control and impress others. A genuinely confident person feels no need to intimidate or be arrogant. Real power comes with authentic self-acceptance, not manipulation. When you live with civility and compassion, you gain far more power. You also move into the synchronistic flow of unity and connection, stimulating the laws of harmony and right action and opening yourself to all the joys and blessings they can bring.

5. Lies of undeservingness, unworthiness, and inferiority: People are taught that they're undeserving for a number of different reasons, but if you've been given this misinformation, you need to know that you're just living according to someone else's false priorities. Your worthiness comes from your Divine legacy; and by virtue of that blessed connection, you're deserving of all the wonderful things the Universe has to offer. Redefinition is absolutely crucial in this case. Let go of the inferiority and the conditional self-acceptance. Free yourself to be yourself and know that you deserve!

6. Lies of acquisition and external value: When you define yourself by your wealth—or lack of it—you'll find that your happiness is on shaky ground. Money may make life easier, but it doesn't make you a better person. It doesn't guarantee acceptance by others, nor should it be the source of your self-approval. This money-based caste system is not only very fragile, it disconnects you from your authentic value and from the value of people at every level of income. Money is fine, but don't make it the only place where you find meaning or worth. When you learn to see value everywhere, you know the greatest acquisition is current appreciation, and that doesn't cost any money at all.

7. Lies of powerlessness and blame: One of the worst things you can do to your energy field is believe that you're powerless in your own life or in the world. Many people have been victimized and made to feel helpless. Some were mistreated as children, a time when they were physically vulnerable and emotionally unaware—and they've dealt with the consequences. Unfortunately, these experiences can cause individuals to firmly believe in their inability to protect themselves or make wise decisions. Their belief in their powerlessness carries their victim mentality and lack of self-actualization forward, causing them to live in total inertia, seeing themselves as victims of others, of God, and even of the Universe itself.

If you're one of these people, it's especially important that you see the truth. Vent any unexpressed emotions and choose conclusions that honor you and give you strength from now on. Reclaim your power and take the action you need to heal and move on. Instead of being a passive observer in your own life, stand up and believe in the strong and courageous person within.

8. Lies of separation, prejudice, and hatred: All the lies we live are painful to the soul, but these go to the root of many of our individual and social problems. Oftentimes hatred and prejudice are modeled for us and seeded deep into our subconscious, so much so that for many people they become absolute truths and a way of life. People learn to hate based on politics, race, religion, culture, gender, weight, poverty, locality, and countless other reasons. But the more separation we create, the more threatened we feel, causing us to long for even greater power and superiority, increasing the disconnect.

Not only is separation from others a serious problem in terms of attraction, it's also a symptom of the separation we feel from our Divine Source. And the more we hate, the wider that gap gets. So if you're living the lie of separation, you need to know that there's no such thing. In energetic terms, we are inextricably connected. What happens to one person happens to all others and what happens to one group affects the entire Universe. The hatred you send to others returns to you and expands in the consciousness of humanity, creating more problems for you and for everyone else. It's time to shift out of this horrific lie and into your soul's intention for unity and expanding love. This is where your truth and authentic power reside.

⚖

The dictionary defines *truth* as originally meaning "loyalty or trustworthiness, genuine in terms of the quality of being true." It's time to be true to yourself, loyal to the brilliant identity that you know resides within. It's time to trust in your genuine self!

None of the preceding lies account for the power and point of view of the soul. None of them represent the untarnished truth that preceded the skewed misinformation that was unwittingly sent your way. Yes, everyone's got a story. Everyone's been given at least some misinformation from people who were unaware. But you can choose to rewrite it now. Do whatever it takes to make the lies that you've been living—big or small—a thing of the past. When you do, you'll connect with the eternal truth of your power and value. And in that blessed and blissful state, your attraction becomes irresistible.

SOULUTION: COGNITIVE RESTRUCTURING

In order to shift the mental and emotional energies that may be blocking your success, you must identify and reverse the lies that you've been living. List the dishonoring or disempowering assumptions that you engage in most, and for each one write down the healthy and empowering response.

Read these positive options often, and remember not to fault yourself if you fall back into the old, false patterns. After all, finding yourself faulty is just another lie that you're trying to reverse. Instead, gently remind yourself that you view things differently now. You are becoming conscious of—and devoted to—the awareness of your value, resourcefulness, deserving, and authentic power. When you catch yourself thinking in ways that deny these things, gently guide yourself back to the truth that honors you. There's amazing power in this conscious choice. In terms of both your happiness and attraction, your truth really shall set you free!

This process, called "cognitive restructuring," gives you the options to choose healthier, more empowering beliefs. Use your journal to make it a part of your life, and always choose the honoring thoughts, until they become your spontaneous reaction. Your old beliefs and habits may be deeply encoded, but you absolutely can turn them around. The following stories reveal that some lies can become important life lessons. Do you think that may be the case for you?

Carol's Story

Carol sought love and approval—not in perfectionism as in Debby's story, but in being a caretaker. She prioritized people pleasing, making others happy, and pretty much doing everyone else's bidding. The lie she was taught to live was well meaning, but totally out of balance. In fact, her lie became her reason for being, and that reason was taking over her life.

Carol was told that a good girl puts others first; does whatever people want; and is totally giving with her time, efforts, and willingness to please. When she grew up, she went from being a good girl to a good wife and mother; and she always put her extended family's needs over her own.

Carol dutifully lived this lie, creating a life full of service and self-sacrifice without question or boundaries. She became so devoted to putting others first that she completely lost her sense of herself. Not only did it *never* occur to her to experience pleasure herself, she'd even forgotten what had brought her joy in the first place.

What she hadn't realized, however, was that she was not only modeling terribly unhealthy behavior for her children, she was also creating a life force of utter self-dismissal. She saw herself as unimportant, and everything she did revealed that she firmly believed she wasn't worth her own time and energy. This was a lie of such magnitude that the Universe couldn't possibly respond with anything favorable. In fact, the very people that she prioritized disrespected and ignored her. Worse than that, Carol found that in her life of servitude and self-dismissal, she was never happy. In fact, she couldn't even remember how that felt.

Carol hadn't realized it, but the motives for her behaviors were subtly self-serving. Sure, her intentions seemed genuine, yet they were actually motivated out of the desperate need to be a good girl and fulfill her parents' expectations to always serve and please. She was driven by a subconscious need for her parents' approval, but her choices were always dishonoring and completely out of balance with her own needs.

When Carol started to set boundaries and limit what she was doing for others, people were shocked. Over time, though, they actually gained a higher respect for her. She realized she didn't need to please people just to gain their approval. She'd replaced her life-consuming lie with a profound understanding of her true worth, and she finally knew that she deserved to give unconditional love, service, and approval to herself.

> **Carol's lie:** *Other people's needs always come first. It doesn't really matter what I need as long as I'm pleasing others.*

> **Carol's truth:** *I am worthy of my own love and attention. I deserve to be happy and honor my needs and preferences. I am responsible for my own happiness, and everyone else is responsible for theirs.*

Carol had been miserable for quite some time, but she never fully realized it because she had been so accustomed to putting other people's happiness first. Unending effort had been her status quo, but it wasn't too late for her to establish a joyous and balanced life for herself. All it took was her choice to start living the truth that she was worthy of pleasing herself first.

Roger's Story

Roger was a rageaholic. His father had been a hot-tempered alcoholic who was constantly critical and angry. Roger saw that his father had intimidated and controlled his mother and other people by resorting to temper tantrums. So Roger carried on that behavior throughout his own adult life. He became excessively critical of his wife, his kids, and others around him, including the employees at work.

He felt justified in his behavior because he considered himself far superior to the timid and submissive people around him. He also noticed that he felt more powerful when he criticized others because their reaction was to just shut down. What Roger didn't realize, however, was that all of this was fraudulent. It was a fake sense of power and superiority because in order to feel good about himself, he needed to make others feel worse. There was no authenticity, just force and fear.

Roger came in for therapy when he was about to lose his second wife due to his incessant criticism and rage. He finally understood that all of his bravado was merely a transparent attempt to compensate for the fact that he'd felt weakened by his own father's criticism and rage. And he began to see that instead of gaining power, he was actually losing it through his outbursts. He'd thought people were respecting him because of his seeming superiority, but he learned they actually found him annoying—and nobody really liked being in his company because they were never sure when he was going to blow.

Roger had been living a lie of false superiority and power mongering. Although it initially seemed to serve him, it actually cost him the respect of his peers and even his loving relationships. He now knew that he wanted to live authentically, arriving at his power in appropriate and civil ways. So he released the lies of aggression and hostility that had defined him for so long, and he moved to the much more peaceful and authentic strength he found within.

> **Roger's lie:** *I'm powerful through my anger. I know I'm superior, and my criticism of others shows it.*

> **Roger's truth:** *My real power comes from within. I love myself and release conflict. I live authentically—respectful of myself and others. Peace and compassion can be powerful to me. I am free.*

Roger hadn't realized that real power comes from peaceful self-acceptance with respectful and genuine self-expression. He had to learn a lot of new behaviors in order to support this new truth, but he was ready to live without hostility. When he did so, he found that his life was much more tranquil and harmonious than it had ever been. He felt real peace and authentic power for the first time in his life.

Love or Lie

Each of these people played a part in a story that they themselves unknowingly perpetuated. They believed in the lies they were told; and their stories of striving, need for control, and anxiety kept on repeating themselves. *This is the problem with living a lie: when you filter everything through assumptions that disempower you, those assumptions become the driving force in both your life and your attraction. An unresisted lie becomes a vortex of receding energy, a vibrational whirlpool that sucks your happiness and your positive intentions into a vacuum of longing and meaninglessness.*

When your life force is based on an undercurrent of lies, inner happiness will always evade you and outer results will never get through. Ultimately, you'll be forced to engage in even more lies to compensate, and the vortex of negative energy will grow.

The biggest falsehood is that there's something to fear. When you move into the peace and value that your eternal definition provides, you start to understand how very misleading your fear and judgment can be. But you can—and must—take steps to release those old distortions and start living your own authentic truth. In fact, if you want to increase your attraction in this world, you must start to make choices from an entirely different place.

Love is at the center of this monumental choice. Every time you break through the fear and false forms of power and choose to live in peace and love, you'll find yourself getting stronger. Instead of a whirlpool of spiraling discontent, your energy will flow outward with the current of easy synchronicity that loving truth provides.

Throughout your life, no matter what you may encounter, you'll always find yourself faced with this important decision—to come from a place of love or fear. In your thoughts, in your beliefs about yourself and the world, and in your myriad choices every day, you will have the option to respond out of love or react out of fear.

When you live in fear, you consistently feel the need to strive, worry, judge, acquire, and compete. Fear-based thoughts are filled with judgment, whether for yourself or others. And you can see how these kinds of choices would deplete and depress you, making it virtually impossible to be happy. Neither your life force, your level of attraction, nor your intentions can thrive when based upon such fearful, desperate energy.

Loving thoughts, however, release judgment and limitation. They are neither passive nor aggressive, because love comes from a place of peaceful acceptance that reaches out to the genuine embrace of your own life and everyone in it. Love surrenders attachment, unites people, and creates peace, shining like a brilliant light for all the world to see. Without a doubt, it is the most magnetic and harmonic vibration of all!

Living your eternal truth returns you to the love you came from long before this life. It means consciously choosing what beliefs you *want* to be real for you. Those healthy assumptions need to originate in a far different place from the source of your lies. They come from the Source of life itself, the eternal Consciousness of infinite creativity.

When you're feeling confused, ask yourself, *What would love feel like in this situation?* If you're able to move out of the self-sabotaging lies that have blocked your way, your new intentions—based in real love—will honor your spirit, ring with authenticity, and align your life with the Universe in joyous and miraculous manifestation.

CHAPTER ELEVEN

LIVING YOUR TRUTH

"Have confidence in the truth, although you may not be able to comprehend it, although you may suppose its sweetness to be bitter, although you may shrink from it at first. Trust in the truth. . . . Have faith in the truth and live it."

— GAUTAMA BUDDHA

There's nothing more important than knowing, living, and speaking your truth—nothing! No outcome, no external achievement, and no amount of wealth can be more valuable than living in the empowerment and genuine peace that your eternal truth can bring. In fact, this entire life and every experience in it is directed by this mandate: *Know and embrace your unlimited value and your life's true meaning.*

This is perhaps the greatest accomplishment that you can achieve—to release the lies that have defined you and the skewed priorities that have motivated you.

When you move to this higher level of existence, you live in an inner harmony that resonates with everything wonderful in the Universe, reflecting the profound directions of your soul.

It takes a great deal of courage and effort to eradicate the misinformation of the past and to live every day of your life in authenticity. Your distorted perceptions may be toxic to you, but they're also bewitching in their familiarity. They offer the false comfort of habit, all the while they're perpetuating the unhappiness in your life.

In this way, old thoughts, beliefs, and views of yourself and the world actually become a compelling addiction, one that weaves itself through your life in an insidious pattern of spontaneous response. You can become very accustomed to the lies that you're unworthy, weak, or inadequate in some way. Over time, these assumptions become a false "truth" that you unconsciously yet readily accept. What you don't realize is that these conclusions of inadequacy have been learned, and although it may take time and a willingness to change, they can—and must—be unlearned.

The Big Addiction

In my nearly 30 years of counseling, I have to say that I've seen my share of horrors in the ways people have been treated. It's especially hard to witness abuse in the most sacred relationship of all—that of a parent and child. It's amazing what people will do to the trusting and vulnerable souls in their care when they're unable to break out of their own lies of fear and lost power. In a bizarre, misguided attempt to alleviate their own pain, they choose to perpetuate their deep pathologies, their words and behaviors ranging from subtle dismissal to unspeakable cruelty.

I once had a client whose mother set her on fire. Another client's father locked him—at the age of three—in a dark root cellar where mice crawled all over him and bit at his feet. I've dealt with many who have survived sexual abuse. And when my own beloved son was at his Russian orphanage, he was often beaten on the back with poison-ivy branches, made to suffer in pain and discomfort for weeks.

Think of the kind of belief system that such horrible hostility creates! A child's natural reaction to such behavior is to assume that he deserves the mistreatment; that he must have done something wrong; and that the world is an unsafe, untrustworthy place.

But even when mistreatment comes in more subtle forms, it can be equally disempowering. A child may be repeatedly dismissed or neglected by a parent who's "busy making money for the family." Others may be criticized and made to feel like failures no matter how hard they try. Lies of unworthiness are born here and remain in power as long as they're unchallenged.

And if these children reach adulthood and haven't dealt with the lies and mistaken conclusions, it only moves their stories of misery forward. Without letting go of the false beliefs and arriving at new and healthy truths, the people who have received such dismissive or even hostile training then pass on their own distortions to those who rely on them for stability and love. In this way, the victims embrace their stories and become the weavers of the lies for the next generation.

Unfortunately, many people become so deeply indoctrinated in their pain and their lack of power that they don't even consider the fact that they have options. Some secretly value their mistreatment, finding a skewed sense of worthiness in their misery, believing that being a victim makes them special in some way. But giving up power is not only a false bid for sympathy, it conveniently frees them from taking any further responsibility in their lives.

When the lies of our learning become our stories, we begin to filter everything through them—and before too long they become a trap. The distortion and sadness live on, covered up by false striving, rage, or rejection. This, in turn, attracts more problems, increasing our negative emotions and energy. It's all transmutable, however, and it's up to each of us to stand up to the lies and heal the patterns—both within ourselves and within the hurtful legacies expanded all around us.

Think about your own history for a moment. What are the patterns that have held you back? Perhaps you've been given some minor misinformation or limitation, no horrible abuse but just enough misperception to distort your reality and completely change things for you. It could be that you're addicted to prejudice, fear, and judgment. Maybe you've been taught to live small—to expect small because life is always hard. Well, life is sometimes hard, but it's definitely a lie to always expect it to be so. Maybe you were taught the biggest lies of all, that you are powerless or valueless, deserving of misery and unable to change it.

Whatever fraudulent belief system may be weaving itself through your days and your destiny, you need to know that you're attaching your identity—and your whole life force—to something false. And this mistaken core energy is powerful enough to lead your life in unwanted directions! It's like looking in the fun-house mirror and thinking that's your real appearance. When it comes to something as important as your beliefs, however, it's not so funny. It's time to shatter the illusions and know that you don't have to live in distortions any longer.

Illusion or Truth—Mastering the Shift

A dear friend of mine once called this earthly experience "the fun house of fear and longing." In some ways, that may be true, but I prefer to think of it as a University of self-mastery. (Isn't it interesting that *Universe* and *university* come from the same root word, meaning *all together?*)

This is the place and time where we all come together for learning and awareness. How you perceive this earthly experience is up to you, and you're being faced with a choice: to continue to live in a maze of darkness and distortion or to move to a higher understanding that resonates with your true identity, the eternal light that chose to come to this experience in the first place.

The solution is always accessible to you, available in your ongoing choice to live in consciousness and soul truth. Such a choice takes courage and the willingness to let go. It starts with the process of opening your view of yourself and seeing the unalterable value there. It then moves on to a radical shift in thinking—from fear to trust, from loathing to reverence, and from judgment to acceptance. All seem to be extreme polarities, but the distance between each is merely the distance from your head to your heart.

No matter what you've been taught, it's never too late to learn and prioritize genuine love! But you must come to these changes and intentions yourself.

It may be difficult—it may even *seem* impossible—but loving choices in thought, word, and deed are always options for you. In fact, only you can make them your new truth.

Whatever you've learned about yourself in the past, you can now take a course in who you *want* to be from now on. Whatever you've suffered, you can become your own source of love. Vent . . . and cast away the pain.

Let go of the false assumptions—and reveal in their place the power, light, and inescapable truth of your infinite value and eternal identity. This is where love begins.

SOULUTION

What each of us must remember—you, me, and every single soul—is that our perfect and eternal stories existed long before the difficulties that set the stage for the personal lies we may now be living. Love is our originating source, and this tender acceptance is what we're meant to live. This is a core truth that lies dormant for most people, one that can become the most powerfully directing force in your life: Whatever does not come from love is ultimately a lie.

If you're perpetuating falsehoods of fear or faultiness, you must firmly choose to leave those lies behind. Your soul knows its truth and power; and that's love in all its variations, including peace, trust, grace, and compassion. Become conscious of these options—in your view of yourself, of others, and of the world itself. In so doing, you can reclaim a new story based in your ancient wisdom and your spirit's understanding. When you do, the lies will fall away and the genuine value of your eternal life will reveal itself in all you do.

Search Engine of the Soul

So what do you do to find this new/ancient truth of yours? The first thing you need to do is calm down and get out of your own way. When you let go of your old ideas about who you were taught to be, you open your heart to finding out who you really are. With this shift from a head-centered to a heart-centered mentality comes the strength of true loving—which is a dramatic shift from the distraction of thinking. Your deliberate intention to take on (and come from) the soul's point of view will help clear your subconscious mind, moving you forward far more dramatically than you ever thought possible.

The Universe will respond to the changes you make—not just in your own life, but in the lives of each and every soul. When you do the inner work to remove fear and judgment from your own heart, your intention and action help remove that negativity from the hearts of everyone. Your intention to heal your false perceptions is supported and expanded in the energetic and spiritual realms. When you make your truth your priority, it will not only change the way you live, it will change life itself.

Your soul is the search engine that can help you find and live your truth. The wisdom available from your higher self is unlimited, and you have free rein to access it all. Use the following four steps to set your new life in motion. There will be such a wonderful difference when you finally start to live your truth that you'll wonder how you could have ever lived any other way.

1. Meditate on your soul's reality. The agitation of your mind is more likely to keep replaying the story you're trying to erase than get you closer to your truth. You need to turn off the mental chaos and go within. Any method of meditation that you enjoy is fine, but whatever form you use, make sure you meditate with the intention to shift into loving consciousness and deeper awareness of your sacred identity.

Open your heart to the sensations of your spirit. Listen for the whispers of wisdom that come your way, and know that you're ready and willing to be enlightened by your eternal mind. Let yourself float between the beautiful sensations of being nowhere and everywhere all at once.

Meditate every day, even if you can only start with a few minutes at a time. Increase the time, and make sure you have no distractions. This is absolutely key to shifting your self-perception, a vital ingredient in creating a happy and harmonious life—as well as an irresistibly magnetic life force.

2. Define yourself according to a higher meaning, one without limit in value, peace, or power. Since your spirit preexisted this life and will continue to exist long after, this is a good place to look for your true definition. You're intrinsically connected to the Divine, the Source of all wonder and abundance. Instead of continuing to define yourself according to the problems and limitations of your old history, you have the option to create a healthy, new perception of yourself, one that is timeless and profoundly true.

Make sure you write down your new truth, your new self-definition, and your honoring beliefs. It's hard to perpetuate a healthy new belief system if all you can remember are the old, negative conclusions. In considering your new definition, look over the many valid and empowering true beliefs that appear later in this chapter. Write down the ones that you feel need the most reinforcing. Carry them with you and read them often. Pick one statement to meditate on for a few minutes each morning and make its truth your intention throughout the day.

3. Aggressively—but lovingly—intervene on your old false beliefs. Since false patterns are addictive, those pesky past perceptions aren't likely to disappear just because you've finally realized they're false. Of course, consciousness is powerful, and your intention to live your truth may instantaneously become real. Don't be surprised, though, if you hear contradictory voices in response to your new intentions. Instead of faulting yourself for your opposing points of view, however, listen to the voice of the enlightened master within. Gently but persistently guide yourself to your new way of thinking.

When in doubt about how to view things or what course of action to take, ask yourself the following questions: *What thought or belief honors me? What choice or point of view brings love and authentic power to me in this situation?*

When you have the answers, muster up the courage to take right action. You can do it. The power of God is within you and behind you in every honoring choice.

4. Replace the conflict within your mind with peaceful and optimistic interpretations. Just as you can approach your life with more peaceful thoughts, you can also choose to approach your thought changes with more peace. When you're faced with two monumentally different frames of mind, don't panic. Ask the questions above, and allow your eternal heart and mind—the enlightened master that's your soul self—to guide you to the replacement thoughts that bring you back to truth, harmony, and authentic power.

Bring your soul into your thinking—and into your approach to everything. A peaceful process brings you far closer to your authentic power than frantic analysis and judgment ever will. So weave the thoughts of your truth and your new self-definition into the fabric of your daily life. Don't hurry; don't worry: *you* are all that you need, and your soul has all the time in the world.

The I of the Storm

SOULUTION

How you define and esteem yourself is the central piece of both your life force and your life experience. Divine presence expresses itself in your core identity, and the unutterable peace and self-love that come from this awareness bring a stability of vibration like nothing else can.

Your spirit's truth is your personal truth. You don't have to live with that split any longer. Walking in the sense of your eternal being changes everything.

Change is the process! Don't just wish you could think differently. Quiet your mind and meditate on healing and heart-centered happiness. Ask for spirit to guide you in all that you think and do. Repeat each new truth often, and don't give up until you feel it deep in your heart.

Thoughts and beliefs are very powerful things. For most of us, it's a major life purpose to master them and bring them to a higher awareness. This raises the energy of the individual (and of the planet) to a loving and powerful intention. Creating an identity based on a spiritual core—along with the beliefs and cognitions that stem from that truth—can shift your life in ways that you never thought possible.

Examine the list of true beliefs that follow. If any seem foreign to you, don't give up—and don't blame yourself either. Just like learning an instrument or a new sport, you have to let yourself practice and experiment until you become a master at it. If you were learning to play the piano, it would be useless to sit and swear at yourself every time you hit a wrong note. Your thinking is the same; the wrong notes are just the lies that other people have taught you. You now have the power and the ability to make your own choices and to live in the energy of your own eternal truth. It's time to harmonize your mind and heart with the real power of your spirit. Practice making each of these beliefs a genuine resonance in your own life force. You'll find within them all that you seek.

True Beliefs

Open yourself to the liberating and empowering force that the following beliefs can bring to your life. It's so important that it bears repeating over and over again: Your view of your worthiness, value, and power is at the center of your truth, your life force, and all that you attract. The beliefs that come from an enlightened understanding of this can bring sustainable peace no matter what may be going on around you. It's up to you to choose these truths and project their energy deep within and far and wide. Meditate on each truth, and feel its vibration filling you up. When you embrace these beliefs with an open heart, you can accelerate through any difficult cycle and shift the events in your life and in the world itself.

— **You are valuable.** Your soul is an eternal source of life-giving light. It shines with a meaning and purpose that you may not be aware of. In fact, your value is so profound that it's impossible in this earthly mind to really understand the extent of your amazing worth. Open to this truth, and affirm the following: *I am valuable; I am eternally valuable. In every experience, I choose to see, know, and honor how truly valuable I am.*

— **You are resourceful.** No matter what you've experienced in the past, you definitely have the resources to deal with what happens in your life—and to make things better. If you've never seen yourself as resourceful before, it's time to know that your abilities come from a higher place. Trust in this and affirm: *I am resourceful; I now recognize the unlimited resources within and around me. I have all that I need to be all that I desire—and to create a happy and fulfilling life right now.*

— **You are worthy.** Your spirit came here to experience wonderful things. You are deserving of those great things—not by virtue of fulfilling some socially acceptable condition, but by virtue of your loving Source—your Divine legacy. You have infinite access to everything valuable. Know that you deserve it and affirm the following: *I am worthy and deserving of all great and good things—I open my heart and my life to receiving them now.*

— **You are powerful.** Even if you've felt relatively powerless in the past, you now need to know the truth. You're a force in the world; your consciousness and energy spread throughout the Universe creating influence far and wide. It's time to step up to your real power and take responsibility for it. Know and affirm: *I am truly powerful, and I have the courage to express my power now. Authentic power is my birthright.*

— **You are eternal.** Your spirit knows—and you can, too—the infinite and cascading energy of your eternal life force. Urgency and fear dissolve when you perceive all things through this understanding. Start to live in the consciousness of unlimited time, and feel the freedom that it brings. Affirm: *I am eternal. I step back and see things from my soul's point of view. All is well.*

— **You have profound inner strength and resilience.** Maybe you haven't felt this way before, but you truly are capable of taking great action and achieving wonderful things. You're resilient, and you have the power to deal with harsh realities; to conquer fear, bounce back, and move forward. Always remember that you can rely on yourself and on the strength that goes back through all eternity. Affirm: *I know I have profound inner strength. I am resilient, self-reliant, and capable of great deeds. I call upon the power within; it is always there for me.*

— **You have a strong intuitive voice and inner wisdom.** Your higher self has access to all of the information you will ever need. Your own spirit longs to guide and inspire you, but you have to believe in this innate power of yours. Slow down, quiet your mind, and get out of your worry; and you'll soon be able to open up to your soul's direction and advice. Meditate often, asking for answers whenever you need them. Affirm: *My intuitive voice guides and directs me. I open myself to the wisdom within; I am inspired and supported in wonderful ways.*

— **You are loved. Now and always, you are loved.** The heart of Divine love is your Source, your friend, and your ever-caring partner in all things. Connecting with this blissful acceptance may seem foreign at first, but the peace it brings is astounding—and living each day in this loving awareness brings solutions to every arena of your life. So meditate on your own heart center and feel the Divine love that resides there. Affirm: *I am accepted, nourished, and loved. I open my heart to the greatest peace of all. Every moment I am blessed with the presence and endless love of the Divine.*

— **You are capable of creating miracles.** Due to this vast and pervasive power of Divine love, your spirit is blessed with magic of all kinds. Every moment brings a new opportunity, and you never know when a shift in consciousness will change your reality completely. Open yourself to the lessons of every experience, and know that something wonderful and unexpected could be right around the corner. See your entire life as a miracle in progress and affirm: *I am capable of magical creations. Every breath is a blessing; every heartbeat is a gift. I open myself to the miracle of now—and to all the miracles to come.*

True Choices

All of these statements are true for you, but it's not enough just to read them in a book. Each one needs to be embraced and engaged in as a way of life. In fact, if you really want to change your energy and influence your destiny, you need to start *living* them consciously every day.

Living your truth means making the decisions of your daily life according to your higher identity. Just as your thoughts are addictive, many of your behaviors and choices are spontaneous reactions as well. So to live your truth in all that you do, you must bring your higher consciousness to all of your choices, big and small.

To honor your truth, you must honor yourself. And your intention to do so must be a guiding directive throughout your day. When making the common and uncommon decisions of your life, ask yourself, *Does this honor me?* Let this be your spirit's mandate: *Does this honor me?*

When you genuinely choose to honor yourself, that reverential energy expands, and your choices will never dishonor others. Sure, you may get some negative reactions when you start to set boundaries and take a higher course. In fact, it may feel risky and unnatural at first. But remember that you're putting aside the old lies and patterns of self-dismissal, so it's going to require courage to chart new territories of action. If you really want to move on to the next level of happiness and manifestation, center yourself in your soul and keep the following guidelines in mind:

1. Make healthy choices in your everyday life. Honor yourself by eating right, getting enough sleep, and getting some muscle movement and relaxation each day.

2. Act with integrity and honesty in your interactions with others. You may be able to make money if you disregard this fundamental part of your truth, but it's a soulless achievement if you lose your dignity to do it.

3. Live a balanced life in all you do, especially in terms of your time and energy. Be sure to set boundaries and make your own life a priority.

4. Take action, make plans. Be flexible, self-directed, and optimistic.

5. Live with reverence for yourself and others. Expect respect, request it, and give it to others in honor of their truth, also.

6. Take time and make time for more meaningful pursuits. Meditate, read, and open yourself to spirit's presence and connection. Believe it or not, this is the windfall you're looking for.

7. Speak your truth. You not only have the right to live it, you have the responsibility to acknowledge it and say it to yourself and the world.

Speaking Your Truth

The manner in which you express yourself is one of the biggest factors in your energetic vibration. This includes your inner self-talk, as well as how you express yourself to others. In terms of your power of attraction, speaking your truth—like knowing and living it—is far more important than picturing your end results. If you continue to dialogue in the lies you were taught, either with yourself or with others, your message of self-deceit will be clear—not only to the Universe, but to everyone around you. You're faced with an important choice here. It's time to open up and speak your truth!

You need to know that even if you've been taught to suppress every genuine emotion, you can change that pattern now. Even if you've been given the lie that you and your opinions don't matter, you can learn how to express yourself now. In fact, both your happiness and your future depend upon this choice. So sing your heart out, and follow these guidelines to help make true expression easier for you:

1. Feel free to vent your feelings in an appropriate way. Write them down or talk to a friend, but get them out so that you don't have to carry their energy with you.

2. Gently, but consistently, intervene on the self-critical or self-condemning thoughts that stop you from speaking your truth to yourself. These perpetuate an enormous lie; and if left unchecked, they can create a powerfully negative momentum in your life.

3. Affirm yourself at every opportunity. Choose to recognize your worth and create an inner dialogue that resonates with the spectacular truth of your eternal value.

4. Express your needs and make reasonable requests in the relationships of your life. You have the right to ask for support; don't be afraid to do so.

5. Learn to express your opinions freely. Your feelings and opinions are both valid and valuable. It's time for you to see the truth in that.

6. Continue to take action on your own behalf. Stand up for yourself! As you leave the lies of the old dramas behind, make sure you don't lose your power in any new drama that develops. You're free to be and express yourself in any situation.

All of these choices honor your highest intention. If you find any of these techniques difficult at first, give yourself permission to practice them and become familiar with the comfort that your truth can bring. In fact, each moment you embrace your truth is a valuable achievement in itself. It's one of the highest, most transformative choices of all. Your old habit of living your lies demonstrated to the Universe that you were willing to immerse yourself in fraudulent energy, making it very difficult to get anything genuine back. But finding and living in your true power changes everything from the inside out.

All this is vitally important in the process of attraction, for it vibrates at the core of life itself. Your soul wants to live in the love and bliss of its eternal expression, and your choice to make that an active part of your life makes you absolutely irresistible. This high resonance connects you with the Universe and with others in beautiful synchronicity and boundless creativity—not only in this life, but in every realm and time.

This isn't just spiritual idealism. This choice to live every moment in your eternal truth completely moves you out of the energies of false striving and desperation. And believe it or not, what you attract will become less and less important to you! *From deep within, the bliss of your truth is the achievement you perpetually seek.* When you finally live it, you will feel no longing, but you'll find that other achievements will follow with ease.

There's real magic vibrating in your soul's eternal power and worth. Know it, speak it, and live its truth now; and you'll find indescribable value in every moment to come.

CHAPTER TWELVE

PUTTING THE PIECES TOGETHER

"I am the soul of the Universe. I am all things, and above all things. I am one without a second. I am pure consciousness, single and universal. I am joy. I am life everlasting."

— SHANKARA

The process of destiny creation is a complicated one. It's clear that there are many influences, and it empowers us to understand them all. We have many personal powers that we can apply to any situation; but it's important to step back and view our lives with clarity, detachment, and a willingness to change. In fact, for most of us, the need for personal change is inextricably linked to our goals for success.

The complexity of the process is what most people miss. All of the laws of attraction indicate very influential patterns in your life, but there's so much more to attraction than meets the eye. Getting what you want isn't like writing some magical letter to Santa. Nor is it a case where saying it enough will make your dreams come true. There's a lot going on. The principles are profound and complex. Your consciousness is a powerhouse, and you need to understand how to use that power in *all* of the events of your life.

So don't give up on the laws—or on the intention to make your dreams a reality. Instead, use the principles to guide you along the way and help you make the kind of lifestyle decisions that will not only bring about specific results . . . but will also create the fabric of a truly complete, happy, and fulfilling life.

The source of all solutions lies within your personal and eternal consciousness. Never forget about the power of your consciousness to create—and change—your reality. In fact, this is the one common denominator that links all of the factors together. Whether you're dealing with life cycles or karma, any of the laws, or even your unknown soul's intention, becoming conscious is the key that unlocks it all. Let's review this phenomenal force in your life, and see all the ways it can help you make the changes you need.

The Power of Consciousness to Live Your Truth

When you understand that it's your entire life force and not just your individual intention that creates your reality, you'll realize the necessity of erasing the lies you've been living by establishing a lifestyle of true beliefs and self-empowerment. It's utterly futile to attach surface intentions for better results to a core of energy depleted by fear, anger, or self-judgment. But you can make this fundamental change to your life force by consistently and consciously choosing your own empowering truth and self-definition. You don't have to live the lies any longer, but you must become aware of them and be willing to change.

People often defend their lies, saying that it's their nature and they can't change it. But if you wallow in conclusions that dishonor and disempower you, you're only defeating every honest intention. You must open up to the truth. Even if your new, optimal belief is the polar opposite of what you've been taught, you can consciously introduce it and make it real for you.

Living your lie means living unconsciously—a choice that significantly throws your power away. When you believe the false stories of your past—whether they're about failure, unworthiness, conditional approval, or anything else—it's guaranteed to sabotage your intention for success. As long as you keep living your story, that story will repeat itself, and you'll be given opportunity after opportunity to learn the inner lessons that this life brings into being.

Remember, however, that the power of the subconscious mind is formidable. It drives us to respond habitually, with little or no awareness of the consequences that our unconsidered responses create. But unhealthy habits are meant to be broken, and when we bring our consciousness to them, we can do just that.

Consider the two columns on the next page. One indicates the patterns of habit; the other indicates more conscious interpretations. Which one of these do you tend to fall into most?

HABIT—AUTOMATIC REACTION	CONSCIOUS RESPONSE
Not noticing what's really going on	Being aware of what you're experiencing and why
Reacting out of habit and emotions only	Remembering your options and your ability to respond differently
Falling into unconscious patterns of escapism, addiction, and shutting down	Choosing behaviors that honor you no matter what's going on
Focusing on what's missing or wrong	Focusing on what you have to appreciate and what's right
Being needy, desperate, or manipulative	Being genuine, authentic, and honestly empowered
Staying stuck, being unwilling to change	Moving forward with a willingness to change and grow

When you look at these lists, you can see why becoming conscious is so important. If you're wondering why things aren't happening the way you'd like them to, it's probably because you're still stuck in some of the automatic reactions. Making the conscious-response choices, however, will be one of the best things you can do to tune into the brilliant life force that will get both immediate and long-term results. The immediate results will be in your daily happiness, and with that kind of energy, the long-term results will follow suit.

People think it's the big decisions of their lives that define them; but it's the daily resonance, the myriad choices we make without thinking, that determine who we are and what we attract. It's time to think about things in a different light. If your daily choices define you, it's time to be conscious of what those choices are.

The Power of Consciousness to Identify, Interpret, and Deal with Any Cycle

Your life, spirit, and karmic cycles are a big influence on what you create and attract. And since every cycle happens for a reason, it's a wonderful opportunity to bring your consciousness to each experience. Instead of ignoring or fighting against the cycle, it's important to see clearly, and to open your mind and heart to the lessons it brings.

Everything—good or bad—is life expressing itself. We came here to experience, and we must be willing to experience it all. Healing—whether physical, mental, emotional, or even financial—comes from opening our hearts and shifting our consciousness to create a calmer and more eternally honest interpretation.

Ultimately, every experience only has the meaning that we give to it. Each event's value is in our response to it—not in the event itself. When we let go of our ego and bring our consciousness to our spirit's point of view, we can comprehend a much higher and deeper meaning. When we establish this clear, unemotional understanding, we become wise to the many wonderful opportunities hidden within each experience. We needn't take anything personally, for from this detached point of view, we can not only achieve peace in the present, but we can also gain guidance about our personal direction.

Check out the following list to see how your powers of choice and consciousness can help you in any phase of any cycle:

1. Cycling in: This is a time in your life when you're going into a new experience—whether it's a brand-new adventure such as going away to college, or perhaps a new period of physical experience that you may even be resistant to, such as menopause. Whatever it is, you can gain more value by bringing your awareness to the beginning of any cycle. Think clearly about what it is you want to achieve in this period of time. In addition to that, consciously decide how you want to emotionally experience it. If you're experiencing or anticipating difficult emotions, you may be making it mean too much. Stop and think about a new way of interpreting things that gives you hope and power instead.

2. Cycling through: When you stay stuck in a problem, the problem grows, but when you go *through* it, it means that you're actually getting to the other side. So if you're going through something, you want to keep the energy optimistic and the momentum going. Reevaluate your options when you're in the middle of this cycle, and continue to take action to support yourself in your ongoing process. Analyze periodically if you're responding out of habit or conscious reaction.

In difficult times, meditate on detachment. Step outside of yourself and sit and watch with unattached knowledge that this cycle will pass into something new. It's a part of your process and you can handle it—from the deepest difficulty to the highest achievement—your eternal life is expressing itself. When you're moving through something, try not to strive so hard against the flow. Instead, see where the current can take you and reflect upon what the Universe can teach you. This willing, detached, and open view of things awakens your consciousness to the will of your spirit's intention. And from this point of view, you know that all things will move you forward according to two main factors: your attitude about it and your action within it.

3. Cycling out: At this point, you realize that things are starting to settle down, and you're moving on to your next phase. A lot of people in this cycle don't think about what's happening next, they're either glad that something difficult is over or sad about a good thing ending. But whether you're cycling out of a happy experience or a difficult one, you still need to bring your consciousness to the momentum of this time. Stop and reflect on what may be coming to an end. Allow yourself to get closure and vent your feelings if the experience warrants it. As you're moving out of one thing, you're also moving into another. Honor the change, let go, and plan the next step on your path.

4. Recycling: Sometimes recycling is not such a good thing—especially when you're repeating difficult patterns! At this phase of cycling, it's especially important to power up your consciousness and find out what's going on. If you see the same pattern over and over again, you know that there's likely a need for some inner change. Even if you've just been stuck in one long-term problem, it may be time to bring a higher consciousness to it. If you're meeting the same critical men, or if you're getting turned down for job after job, ask yourself, *What is the lesson here? What is my soul asking me to focus on?*

In the first case, you may be attracting critical men because you're still engaged in the habit of criticizing yourself. This is an important consciousness lesson—it's time to focus on your value instead of your old lies. The second case may also refer to negative life-force energy, and you may be rejecting yourself in some way. Or perhaps your desperation has led you into the toxic energies of paradoxical intent. If this is the case, you need to remember that part of your power of consciousness has to do with your interpretation. You can make each event seem like the end of the world, becoming more and more desperate all the while. Or you can see the experience as something that may be difficult but which is just a part of your process, awakening you to the option to trust, be flexible, and turn to the courage of your eternal life.

Whatever challenge you may be experiencing, you *do* have the power to get through it, to stop the recycling, and to understand. Since your greatest control comes from what you choose to be conscious of, your most enlightened and empowering approach can be found in your response. To break the pattern of repetition, ask yourself what honors you. Dig deep, and be open to your spirit's answer. It may be difficult, but follow the guidance you're given. Step out of your comfort zone, choose faith instead of fear, and reclaim your power now.

⚖

All of these phases of cycling are part of the ins and outs and ups and downs of life. Although you may not be able to control everything that happens to you, you can always control your reactions. This function of consciousness creation can help you move through the events of your life with power and grace. Review the cycling steps in Chapter 9, use your journal, and meditate on the meaning and the options that each cycle holds for you. When you ignite the power of your eternal consciousness, you can remain peaceful in the eye of the storm.

The Power of Consciousness and Thought

Although the core of your eternal vibration is your spirit's powerful identity, the center of your consciousness in this earthly experience is *thought.* Of course your spirit is still there, and awakening to that presence is a vital resource that you can no longer dismiss—for even this can help you break through your thoughts and enjoy greater feelings of happiness.

Our experiences in this thing we call life, however, weave a web of mental activity that never stops. This is why releasing the lies and arriving at an honoring and empowering truth is so important. With this as our core starting point, we can then go on to consciously determine the quality of our mental experiences and action.

It's through thought that we form our perceptions, and through thought that we express ourselves. Our thoughts form our beliefs, our expectations, and even our emotions. In this way, consciousness is where everything begins. One might even ask, "Where would the world be without thought?" According to the theory of consciousness-created reality, it wouldn't *be* at all. That's how amazing this part of our life experience is. Our thoughts have the power to create miracles, and they're equally able to cause misery as well.

I know I spent much of the first four chapters of this book encouraging you not to get too crazy over your thinking. I still stand by that suggestion because getting crazy over anything is just another way to mess up your thinking! Since thoughts are so powerful, the way you approach them can't be obsessive, urgent, or judgmental—or your intention to change them will just be a waste of time.

The interesting thing about thoughts is that they're most creative when you're relaxed. They're least creative and least connected to the Universal mind when you're worried or upset.

I learned this firsthand in the early years of my counseling practice when I specialized in the treatment of phobias. In all the time since then, I've worked with hundreds of clients who had hugely catastrophic fears that haunted them through their waking hours—and well into their dreams. They feared things such as heart attacks, cancer, aneurysms, and plane and car crashes, just to name a few of the worst-case scenarios that plagued their minds. And for most of these people—at least at the beginning of their therapy—these fears were chronic and intense everyday occurrences. In spite of that, their specific fears didn't materialize. In fact, in the 30 years and hundreds and hundreds of phobics I've dealt with, only one person has died from the thing she was afraid of, and even in that one case I don't believe that her fears made it a reality. Now you'd think, even just considering the statistics alone, that the coincidence of occurrence would have to be much higher than that.

So what's going on with this *thoughts are things* philosophy? Well, it comes down to a matter of *brain frequency.* Your thoughts are the most creative when you're in a relaxed state and your brain frequency is at what's called *alpha level,* which is 7 to 14 cycles per second. This is why hypnosis, relaxation, and guided visualization are so important. These techniques put you in a tranquil state where your mind frequency will settle down, and you can create the mental images and programming of your affirmations and intentions.

However, when your brain frequency moves up and out of alpha into the *beta* range, which is above 14 cycles per second, your mind's creative power is greatly reduced. The more worry and anxiety you feel, the higher your brain frequency rises, and the less productive your thoughts become.

This explains why so many people like phobics and obsessive compulsives can worry so much and not have their specific fears come true. They do experience expanding anxiety, however, because their negative focus consumes them and they devote themselves to their lies of needing control and safety. I've had, of course, other clients whose issue-related fears *did* materialize. In fact, I deal with them all the time. For example, a woman might repeatedly think she'll never find a man, and that could be entirely true. But I would wager that more than her specific fear, it's her life force of desperation that's causing the outcome she dreads.

So if thoughts are the core of your consciousness, and your consciousness creates your reality, what's the best approach to changing your thinking? The answer is a sane, balanced, self-loving attitude that focuses on the issues that matter most. This balanced approach doesn't dismiss the importance of staying positive, yet it also doesn't mean you have to obsess about your thinking and freak out over any negative conclusion that may flash through your mind. This centered approach also provides a much more peaceful filter through which you view your process of manifestation. You can build an ongoing awareness of your cognitive resonance, while giving yourself the freedom and flexibility to investigate other patterns that may need your attention, also.

Review the *Soul*utions in Part I, but when it comes to your thinking, remember the following guidelines:

1. Your most important thought changes will be to identify and switch the negative lies of your past, especially those that deplete or dishonor you. Your self-view is vitally important to the process of consciousness creation because it changes your whole life force and everything else in the process.

2. Intervene on other mental patterns of limitation or fear. When you notice yourself being fearful or pessimistic, *gently* remind yourself you don't have to think in that way any longer. At the very least, release the worries; but if you can, replace them with a simple thought that brings optimism and trust.

3. Practice positive thoughts of affirmation, appreciation, and peace. Write down your positive options and repeat them often. Remind yourself that these statements represent your truth.

4. Meditate on your affirmative thoughts so that you can experience them in the alpha state. Pick a simple, short affirmation, such as *I am worthy,* or *I am love,* and use it as a peaceful mantra to lead you into meditation or sleep. Just repeat it softly and lovingly with no urgency or outcome attached.

By taking this loving and peaceful approach to retraining your thinking, you reduce desperation and raise your consciousness to higher intentions. You also harmonize with the shared consciousness of the universal mind—an alignment that helps to stimulate the laws.

The Power of Consciousness and the Laws

If you really want to activate the laws of attraction in your life, you need to know how to employ your personal powers of energy and conscious intention in ways that will resonate with their creative force. Keeping the following principles in mind will go a long way toward helping you create the destiny you desire.

1. The Law of Manifestation—how you create: Your consciousness creates your reality and that's based on your life force. Let go of the lies that are swimming around in your subconscious and conscious mind; and instead of focusing on what's wrong, focus on what's right with you and your life. At every opportunity, return your consciousness to the unimpeachable truth of your value, worthiness, and eternal identity.

2. The Law of Magnetism—how you attract: This is all about energy, so be aware of the emotions you live in. Love yourself through them. Remember to choose trust instead of fear and peace instead of conflict. Make these conscious intentions matter!

3. The Law of Pure Desire—how you intend: Become aware of why you desire your goals, and be honest about your motivation. Take the ego out of your intention. Satisfy your need for happiness yourself, and work on your plans in present peace.

4. The Law of Paradoxical Intent—how you attach: Are you conscious of any desperation in your life? If so, you need to relax and let go of control. Rein in the urgency and need, and allow yourself to approach your desires with calm and flexible determination. No matter what you're working on, keep your eye on present appreciation.

5. The Law of Harmony—how you connect: Become conscious of the oneness of all. The unity we share isn't just spiritual; it's energetic and even scientific. Stop seeing yourself as separate or as superior or inferior. When you consciously connect in this harmonious equality, you accelerate positive creation beyond measure.

6. The Law of Right Action—how you interact: Your undeniable connection requires you to become more aware of your actions toward others. Live with integrity and compassion. Bring love to every person and experience. Say it, send it, choose it, be it.

7. The Law of Expanding Influence—how your energy expands and returns: This is the master system—your energetic connection to universal mind (and to all people) expands your consciousness far and wide. Become more aware of the impact you have on others and of their influence on you. You have power in both directions. Use it wisely!

All of the laws require you to become more conscious in your daily life, and that takes time. Turn on your intellectual awareness; and stop living merely out of emotion, ego, and reaction. The power of your consciousness is unlimited in terms of your ability to create, but you have to employ it in your daily life in order to make a difference. You already have the keys to unlock that door!

The Six Keys to Consciousness Creation

If you want to enhance your ability to create consciously, there are things you can do on a regular basis to make that happen. Implement the following six techniques in little and big ways, and you'll soon see that abundance can be a present experience and not just a future goal.

Key 1: Relaxation and Meditation

When you understand the significant connection between brain-wave frequency and personal creation, you'll realize that you're going to have to slow down and relax. In order to be more productive in creating your goals and a happy life force, you need to lower your brain-wave frequency in a relaxed state on a regular basis. This will help you quiet your mind—an important part of consciousness shifting—and relax your body, producing the more magnetic vibrations of peace and calm. In understanding this, you know that no matter what form of meditation you use, the mere practice of it stimulates the first two laws of attraction immediately.

But there's more to meditation than that. If you use your meditation time not only to relax but also to release, you can accelerate your shift in consciousness from the old patterns of your story to your new and expanding truth. After you relax, visualize any old information, hurts, or issues slowly lifting out of your body, becoming a cloud that drifts away on the wind until it finally disappears. Bless your past and let it go.

You can also meditate on a word, intention, or short affirmation. As you relax, breathe deeply and simply repeat the word or statement you want to reinforce. Repeat statements such as: *I am love, I am healthy, I am deserving, I am valuable, I am eternal.*

Remember, your time of quiet mind is the most powerful and productive of your day. So if you really want to introduce these life-changing truths into your subconscious mind, you not only need to affirm them in your alert, waking state, you need to keep planting the seeds when you're relaxed. Finally, meditation is the one time when you can shut out the outside world and reconnect with your own eternal spirit. This still point of connection to the loving presence of God, angels, spirit guides, and your own higher self is of such inestimable value in consciousness creation that it simply can't be dismissed.

Focus on the light of your own heart center. Feel the power and peace that your Source and eternal spirit can bring you. Ask for information and be willing to receive. The more you do so, the more connected you'll feel, getting ideas and inspiration in the waking state as well. You'll be amazed by the wonderful effect that this one technique can have on your life.

Key 2: Affirmation

As you can tell, leading an affirmative life is a key part of unlocking the mysteries of dynamic destiny creation. It's interesting that many books tell you not to talk negatively, but then go on to say that affirmation doesn't work! But if you bring your consciousness to it, you always have the option to affirm instead of negate.

Affirmation can be applied in two ways: The first is a regular and systematic approach. This is where you write your affirmations down, read them often, and meditate on their truth and meaning. The second way is as a tool for intervention. When you notice that you're having a persistent negative thought, remind yourself of your positive option. Make a releasing statement and let it go. If the same old issues keep coming up, do the cognitive-restructuring technique described in the previous chapter, and use those replacement thoughts as affirmations and new intentions for you.

Remember to frame your affirmations in ways that resonate with your heart. If you resist saying *I love myself,* start by saying *I'm learning to love myself; I'm opening to loving myself more and more each day.* As time goes on, introduce the more absolute thoughts and let yourself get comfortable with them. Keep in mind that if you do these in a relaxed state, it will be easier and more effective to change the undercurrent of your subconscious mind.

Affirm yourself, but don't stop there. Affirm your life, saying: *Today is a beautiful day,* then take a moment to notice that. Also affirm your future. This initiates optimism and positive expectations—a very powerful resonance in your energetic vibration. Take a deep breath and say, *My life is getting better and better all the time—and I have the power to create happiness now. I am excited about the adventure each new day brings and about all of the unexpected blessings coming my way.*

Affirmation is never false and never a waste of time. You may not immediately see results, but don't forget about the power of life-force vibration. As you integrate these positive views, you'll accumulate the matching energy there, and that's a consciousness you want send out to the world.

Key 3: Visualization

Imagery is a huge part of consciousness creation! Consistently looking at negative images and conjuring up horrible pictures in your mind can have a very unhealthy affect on your encoded consciousness and can wreak havoc on your ongoing life force. Peaceful images, however, create gentle vibrations in your energy and are more likely to effectively impact the reality you create.

So surround yourself with beautiful artwork—then take the time to appreciate it! Make conscious decisions about what you watch on television. Try not to watch violent programming or the news right before bed because studies indicate that those final images and thoughts before sleep are repeated throughout the night. They not only impact the quality of your sleep, but also the content of your dreams and consciousness.

In terms of visualizing your desired end results, remember to meditate and relax a bit first. In this relaxed state, your images of achievement have much more creative power. Don't obsess, however. If your visualization becomes urgent, it immediately moves you out of alpha brain frequency and into the less fruitful state of beta.

In addition to attaching your mental images to relaxation, it's extremely attractive to attach them to the energy of appreciation. A wonderful technique recommended by my friend Reverend Jason Borton, intuitive coach, involves a vision board. He suggests that instead of limiting your vision board to images of the good things you want in the future, also add pictures of the wonderful things you already have in your life. Whether it's photos of your kids, your home, your garden, or your favorite vacation spot, put them along with the images of your anticipated happy results. As you look at your vision board, you'll see all the things that you already love in your life, and it will stimulate a resonance of appreciation. Then when you scan the other images of your desired end results, your energy of gratitude will expand, transferring to those things that have yet to come. In this way, you're actually charging your expectations with the emotions of fond memories and present appreciation. In terms of your energy and the universal response, there will be a subtle, psychic acknowledgment that all of these things are already taking place.

Key 4: Gratitude

Appreciation is a state of emotional consciousness that most people limit to the special events in their lives. Unfortunately, this attitude seriously hinders their ability to be happy and create a magnetic life force. It also reduces the energy of appreciation shared in the consciousness of humankind—spreading an undercurrent of discontent that seems to be growing. More and more people seem to be living in envy of what others have instead of joy and gratitude.

But if you look very closely, you can find value in *everything* from a fleeting moment of leisure to the simple scent of a flower. This constant awareness of a thankful heart is one of your most positive and powerful tools of attraction. More than that, the choices of gratitude and love will always bring you closer to your soul's intention, an alignment that means more than you might think.

Gratitude happens in two important ways: first in the intention to recognize and appreciate value, second in the intention to create it. The act of creating value can be a real source of happiness, combining joy and positive purpose, bringing present awareness to ongoing choices. It's more than *looking* for things to be grateful for; it's actively *creating* things to be grateful for!

This intention to appreciate creates a brilliant life force that draws more to appreciate. Look around and say, *I'm really grateful for that,* or *I appreciate this.* Stop for a moment to feel the sensations, breathe in the appreciation, and recognize the gratitude growing in your heart. Look at your loved ones and take time to be thankful. Reflect on the value they bring to your life and make a point of expressing your love and thanks.

Also, look in the mirror and say, *I appreciate myself. I am grateful for all that I do for myself each day and am grateful for my time and attention.* Acknowledging and appreciating the value of your true self establishes an internal strength and sense of deserving that gives you the power to deal with any obstacle that may arise. This is the part of you that's unshakeable and unstoppable. It's time for you to be grateful for your eternal life and finally see the value in that. When you do, you'll recognize and be thankful for all the blessings that your birthright can bring you.

Gratitude is a whole-life attitude that rings with the truth and wisdom of seeing things clearly. In every decision to see value, create it, and feel thankful for it, your appreciation aligns your life resonance with the source of all things wonderful. Gratitude for all that you are and all that you have is a tender and healing vibration, so appreciate deeply and often!

Key 5: Love

Love isn't just a romantic attachment; it's a powerful and creative force in the Universe. In terms of a fulfilling life and vibrant life force, the consciousness of love is the energy that ignites it all. This isn't just a fanciful ideal. It's an energetic truth.

Love is the heart-centered energy that connects us and forges meaning out of mere existence. We're motivated by the things we love; we're thrilled, compelled, and grateful. The emotion of love can be kindled by appreciation for a person, a place, or even an experience—such as a warm summer day, the sound of music, the vision of a field of flowers, or the beauty of a piece of art. Whatever it may be, when we love something or someone, it fills our heart with joy and our life with meaning.

Love expands in a vortex of vibrating energy, and you're at the eye of that swirling force. You not only deserve your own love, you're solely responsible for it. If you don't choose to love yourself and see all the value you possess, it will be impossible for that vortex to pick up the momentum it needs to reach outward and create the effects you desire. The agony of self-loathing—or even mere self-dismissal—becomes a filter through which you experience everything else, poisoning your potential joy and making it next to impossible to be truly happy. So if self-love remains a foreign concept to you, you need to know that you're still living someone else's lie, and you have the option to embrace a new truth right now.

Your self-loving consciousness expands when you remember to intend it elsewhere as well. As you go through your day, notice all the ways you can bring the energy of love to your life. Repeat the word *love* as you look at the people, things, and events around you. You'll automatically feel the release of tension, softening the vibration of your life force and creating a much more irresistible resonance. The intention to love is one of the most dynamic approaches you can take toward resolving any problem or securing any solution. If somebody is bothering you, send that person love. If a situation seems impossible, send it love. If you're feeling stuck in a cycle or just plain down, send love to yourself. The energy of love is creative and powerful. This is where the magic happens, so instead of dismissing it, let it become the thing you do best.

Loving intention can enhance your energy so much that your life becomes a joyous place that you just love to be in. Think about being happy every single day! Bringing love to your consciousness is the way to make that happen.

It's clear that this consciousness shift is a truly life-changing point of view. Love yourself, love the people in your life, the places you go, and the things you do. *When love becomes the filter through which you view your reality, the change is so dramatic that you'll never see anything in the same way again.*

Key 6: Awareness and Choice

You can bring a higher awareness to every aspect of your life. Gently but persistently choose to become more conscious of your thoughts, your choices, and all of the options available to you in any circumstance.

If you're moving through life with blinders on, you're letting your emotions and your ego determine your destiny. With no consciousness brought to the present moment, it will be impossible to consciously create the future you want.

Stop and think about the mental and emotional energy of your life. If you're still lingering in any lies about your power, value, or deservingness, you need to bring your awareness to your cognitive options. Don't panic; just remind yourself whenever you can that you do have the opportunity to choose thoughts and reactions that honor and empower you. When you make informed choices, you master your thoughts and emotions.

In science and in life, the concept of *adjacent possibilities* reveals that no matter what predictable outcome may be expected, there's always the chance that something entirely different may happen, expanding the opportunity for diverse and unexpected changes. In terms of your personal experience, this means that you're never limited by your old definitions. Your life and your consciousness are evolving all the time. Every moment there are dozens—even hundreds—of adjacent possibilities, countless options for perception, thought, and action that can completely alter your reality. Become aware of them! A purposeful shift in focus could result in unexpected surprises; and one moment of moving into an adjacent possibility could lead your life into unknown and vastly different directions.

Remember that the joy or misery of any event comes from how you consciously interpret it. No matter what is going on, within your awareness is the ability to recognize a higher meaning. Don't be blindsided by distractions, distortions, or disappointments. Resolve to stay conscious and open your heart and mind to all the positive options within and around you.

If you want to know the truth, this is where virtually all your power lies. You can't recognize love if you're not conscious of its presence. You can't feel appreciation if you remain unaware of what you have to be thankful for. Options, imagination, optimism, trust, and love are all waiting in your consciousness field. Become aware of these alternatives, and then muster up the courage to choose them. As you continue to make these choices, it will become easier and easier to make them a way of life.

All over the world, people are realizing that they can no longer live according to old rules and patterns. I'm sure you can feel it, too. You know in your heart that it's time for a change—and that change is *consciousness*. To shift it in the world, you must shift it in yourself. Smile; and know that as you do so, you're changing your own destiny, as well as the future that we all share.

True Beliefs

There are many roads we can follow on our journey of destiny creation. In our process, if we find that one option doesn't take us in the best direction, we can always take a different path. If one technique doesn't produce the desired results, we can investigate and find out why. We can explore what else may be going on, and by obtaining all the facts, we become empowered. In experience after experience, it's not so much what happens to us, but how we *respond* to what happens that moves us forward to create our future. When we learn to respond in healthy ways, we create value at the core of our consciousness, and the joyous Universe returns healthy and happy results.

The power to change everything is found in the choice to change beliefs. But that change must be gentle and pervasive, not desperate or needy. Believe in yourself and in your future. The stronger your faith in your own capabilities and worthiness, the stronger your energetic momentum in the world.

This is why breaking away from any false self-perception is so important. You may have a history, but you are *not* that history. Just because someone you love taught you something when you were young, that doesn't make it true. It's time to clear away the dust and the dirt of your old false fears and shed light on the darkness that's been living there. Meditate on your own self-love and eternal worthiness every day. This isn't a waste of time; it's the inescapable truth that will finally set you free.

Consciousness does create, and your consciousness is capable of creating great wonders. You have the power to arrive at this magnificent state whenever you rise above the chaos and rest within your heart and soul. The abundance you long for is within you right now. It's in every choice and every loving thought.

In each moment, your life is expressing itself, and your spirit wants you to remember the dazzling beauty of your truth. Stop the striving and listen to the whispers of wisdom reaching up from your eternal soul. The answers, the joy, and the blessings you seek are all available there.

EPILOGUE

Legacy of Love

"Consciousness empowers us to experience the oneness in everything and everyone."

— DR. DARREN R. WEISSMAN

Life moves through pain and pleasure in dazzling ways, the depths of one accentuating the heights of the other. Is it possible to go through these two extremes at the same time? There's no doubt in my mind that it is—in fact, I have recently visited this state of emotional polarity myself. It's a fragile but powerful place to be, a bittersweet moment of intensity.

In the Introduction, I talked about my beloved friend Pat, who'd contracted ALS and whose experience was a major inspiration for this book. A short time ago, Pat's spirit let her physical form go and moved on to a very different vibration. In her life and death, she showed me that in spite of great difficulty, you can still experience unspeakable joy. And even now, as I find myself crying over my friend's passing, through all of the tears and mourning I can still feel such profound appreciation and utter bliss when I sense the presence of her life force in mine.

Knowing Pat has been one of the greatest blessings of my life. She called me her teacher, but it turned out that she was mine. Throughout her life, she taught me about the power of laughter and abiding love. And in the last year of her life, she taught me more about grace, wisdom, and eternity than I'd ever known before.

Pat hadn't been able to move for quite some time; but amazingly, she was still able to be blissfully happy, and she communicated that in no uncertain terms. Of course, it had taken her some time to process her experience and develop a consciousness that transcended the difficulty of it all. But she eventually arrived at a place where she could find a purpose that was genuinely valuable to her—and to all of us who knew her.

Pat told me she'd been traveling in her sleep, and she knew that her soul would live on. She was unafraid because she'd awakened to the spirit within and to the reality of her eternal life. She only wished she'd connected with that inner self in a more significant way before. But in her enforced immobility, she meditated and was able to let go and experience something greater than this earthly realm. In this way, she found deep meaning not only in her situation, but also in her life and physical death.

There was a sense of enlightenment about her. She'd always been enormously funny, and even in illness, she never lost her sense of humor. She had also always been exceedingly loving; but in those last years, the love she emanated filled every space around her and spread across the Universe in palpable waves.

No matter what, Pat had the power to appreciate everything—although she couldn't even move. Every little thing and memory could bring her joy. She was not a victim or a taskmaster. And although she had times of frustration and sadness when she thought of what she'd leave behind, she always returned to the peace of her profound spiritual perception.

I don't know all the reasons why her eternal spirit led her down this path. Something that big certainly seems like a life lesson. Perhaps it was the ultimate letting go of attachment. Perhaps it was her intention to show those of us who knew and loved her that happiness is achievable in virtually any situation.

I know that through all my tears and all the grief, there was a great gift in the lessons she gave me. She taught me that there's never any need to wait to be happy. She taught me to embrace every moment and to open myself to the gratitude that could be taking place if I could just relax and let the peace and appreciation in.

I've spent my whole life teaching people how to redefine themselves and their situations, but I never saw the unlimited truth quite so clearly until I saw it through Pat's eyes. We have so many options in every moment—*unlimited* options. Instead of being annoyed by the little disruptions, we can find joy there. Instead of seeing our daily tasks as tedious or burdensome, we can do them with the knowledge that this, too, is our life expressing itself. And instead of longing and discontent, we can look around us and say, *My life is the gift; now let's see what joyful places I can take it to.*

In spite of everything—maybe because of everything she went through—Pat found that joyful place. She shared that joy with me, and it's my greatest desire and pleasure to share it with you. She isn't separate from us—although you may have never known her in this earthly form. Each and every consciousness connects in very real energetic terms, and this collective connection cannot be deterred.

In terms of energy and consciousness, Pat is still very much alive. Her life force expands all over the Universe, joining with others of like energy to create real consequences in the world. Now, you may think that's merely because her spirit is free to roam, but this power of distant influence isn't limited to the spirit realm. Right now your energy is just as influential. There's no separation between the individual soul and the global spirit—and the consciousness that we as a species share is a force to be reckoned with.

We Are Family!

Scientifically speaking, there's no doubt about our energetic connection. We aren't isolated individuals whose only impact is on our immediate family and friends. We work together every day, contributing to the consciousness field that is the entire human race.

In her book *Everything You Need to Know to Feel Go(o)d,* Candace Pert, Ph.D., described the vitality of our connection so well:

> Consider that we're all part of a resonating network, connected not by rigid wires, but by a flow of pulsating energy passing through our vibrating molecules of emotion—receptors, peptides, and other informational substances—as they bind. Yours, mine, those of the person sitting next to you, and so on, creating one energetic, resonating field.

This beautiful "resonating field" that is the consciousness of the human race is awash with the energy and information that we pour into it every day. We also feed off it, picking up certain types of vibrations and feeling their influences in subtle and not so subtle ways. The kind of resonance we're most likely to pick up is determined by two main factors:

1. Our personal consciousness and our own energetic predisposition

2. The power and momentum of the field's most prevalent energy at any given time

Collective feelings and attitudes are floating through our environment, permeating our own subconscious minds and emotional realities. If those drifting feelings are negative, we're more likely to pick them up if we ourselves are going through a pessimistic attitude. If, on the other hand, we're experiencing something pleasant or just perceiving things more optimistically, we'll be much more likely to sense the loving vibrations in the field.

The second influence on consciousness expansion is the power and momentum of the shared dominant energy. A major event or series of events can project a certain kind of resonance, and as more and more people become exposed to the experience, that energy accumulates and grows stronger with each person's emotional response.

One such example happened on September 11, 2001, when the World Trade Centers in New York City were destroyed, the Pentagon was damaged, and a plane crashed in Pennsylvania due to terrorist attacks. The experiences themselves, along with the cascading emotional effect of people's reactions to them, created a powerful momentum that was felt around the globe. The images of those horrible events were repeated hundreds—even thousands—of times in the media all over the world. And since imagery is a big part of consciousness creation, that kind of potent visual couldn't help but have a huge effect on the minds and hearts of those who witnessed it, eventually shifting the energy of the entire planet.

It was difficult seeing those images without having a severe emotional reaction. Long after the shock of the events set in, the fear was still expanding, becoming deeply indoctrinated in the consciousness of individuals and of the human race; and in many ways, it's expanding still.

Regarding this and several other issues, we feel the consciousness of each and every person. In recent times, the energy of worry has been expanding. Whether it's worry about the economy, the environment, or national safety, the field of fear is being well fed.

On a personal basis, you need to know that you don't have to buy into the mass reaction. If you've gone through something difficult yourself, such as the loss of a job, you need to vent the emotions around that; but you don't have to sit around talking about how hopeless things are. You don't have to define yourself by the experience or by the group mentality. You're free to create a new consciousness—one of resilience, hope, and determination. You can gather with people of like intention to meditate, pray, act, and affirm together.

The truth is that we all need to take this kind of action for ourselves and for the world. Instead of getting caught up in the consciousness of fear, we can join forces to move the world into the higher vibration of loving consciousness. In fact, I believe that many of us have been brought together in this time and place for precisely that reason. You and I and millions of souls have all shared a spiritual intention to heal the fear and bring unity out of separation.

But we can't release the competition between nations and cultures until we release it among ourselves. It's time to let go of the hostility and striving and make compassion and personal peace a priority instead. Whatever your personal goals, your soul has a very specific plan for you. That goal will fit with the grand spiritual intention: to move you and the world forward on the path to higher purpose and understanding, to expand love and harmony, in essence to become one—again.

We've been through difficult times as a species before. Wars, depression, environmental changes—we've survived a lot, and as a group we can help make the changes that are needed now. We must dig deep into our spiritual truth to find the faith, trust, and perseverance that can carry us through. This isn't just a fanciful idea; it's a genuine intention that can change *everything*.

Listen closely to your eternal voice. It lives within you, perennially whispering the truth of your value, worthiness, and phenomenal power. When you bring this stunning realization into your daily routine, every element of your life will transform. Spend a few minutes each day aligning yourself with this ultimate truth, then continue to direct that healing and loving intention into the bright and open field of human consciousness. Do this often, and the vortex will grow.

None of us know what interesting turns our lives may take. Whatever we do or achieve, we place our imprints on this world—a consciousness footprint that leaves its mark on our collective destinies—and on the entire Universe. We are capable of great miracles, and love is the greatest miracle of all. If we can make it the center of our approach to ourselves and others, a shining new reality will be revealed.

The Love Club

Let's connect our loving intentions to create a vortex of influence for ourselves and everyone else. Energy expands, and shared energy expands exponentially. If we all commit to a simple prayer of focused love every day, we could change everything! Affirm: *I choose love! For myself, for others, for the world itself, I choose love!* Say this heartfelt intention often, and know that together we are sharing and expanding love in all directions, providing wonderful consequences beyond our wildest dreams.

Such is the power of love consciousness! It can redefine us and give us wings. It can raise us up and transform adversity. Pure love can create healing and happiness beyond comprehension. And when we focus on this wonderful energy, we can bring our world to a brand-new, beautiful place. That spectacular destination is beckoning, and love is the vehicle that will take us there.

ACKNOWLEDGMENTS

Deep appreciation for the caring, supportive love of my family—Sarah Marie Klingler; Benjamin Earl Taylor, Jr.; Sharon Klingler; Vica Taylor; Jenyaa Taylor; Ethan Taylor; Devin Staurbringer; Yvonne Taylor; Kevin and Kathryn Klingler.

Unending gratitude for the incredible people at Hay House, including Louise Hay, Reid Tracy, Jill Kramer, Jessica Kelley, Jacqui Clark, Richelle Zizian, Christy Salinas, Diane Ray, Emily Manning, Amy Gingery, and *all* of the lovely people at this wonderful publishing company.

For the tireless effort, industry, and creativity of my business manager, Noreen Paradise; and for the long hours and late nights, and always good humor of my typist, Rhonda Lamvermeyer; and the funny Andrea Lonshine.

To my inspiring colleagues: Candace Pert, Mike Ruff, Wayne Dyer, Colette Baron-Reid, Darren Weissman, Eldon Taylor, Deborah King, Donna Eden, David Feinstein, Peggy McColl, John Holland, Carmen Herra, John C. White, Lauren Mackler, and Tom Newman.

To the family of my heart: Marilyn Verbus, Barbara van Rensselaer, Ed Conghanor, Julianne Stein, Melissa Matousek, Tom and Ellie Cratsley, Karen Petcak, Michele Dregas, Valerie Darville and Julia White, Esther Jalylatie; and Delores, Donna, and Kathy Maroon—so much love to you all.

To my Lily Dale family: Sue Glasier, Joanne Taft, John White, Stephanie Turachak, Barbara Sanson,

Alpha Husted, Ellie Cratsley, Martie Hughes, Lynne Forget, Shelly Takei, Connie Griffith, Elaine Thomas, Jaccolin and Joanne Franchina, Tim Brainard, Carolyn Sampson, Jessie Furst, and Neal Rzepkowski.

To the wonderful coaches, consultants, and counselors I've worked with, including Michael Freedman, Tom Cratsley, Mariana Cooper, Kathy Atkinson, Kate Beeders, and especially Jason Borton, who shared his ideas for his appreciation/vision board with me.

A very special thank-you to my friends at the Tivoli Lodge, Diane and Bob Lazier, and Mark Asoian. Thanks for giving me a beautiful place to write in the summer and stay in the winter when I'm skiing the spectacular slopes of Vail, Colorado.

And speaking of Vail, thank you to the great people at Unity of the Mountains, and to all of the Unity churches where I've had the privilege to speak. It has always been a great pleasure.

To my spirit family: Anna and Charles Salvaggio, Ron Klingler, Rudy Staurbringer, Earl Taylor, Chris Cary, Pat Davidson, Flo Bolton, Flo Becker, Tony, Raphael, Jude, and of course the Divine Consciousness that lives in all things and loves in all ways.

Finally, I want to thank *you* so very much—all of you who have shared your beautiful energy and support in so many ways and who have brought so much value to my life. And I want you to know that your loving connections have meant more to me than I can ever say. It is my hope that we can all share a caring intention with and for each other, joining together to expand the consciousness of love, compassion, and truth throughout the world. May bliss and blessings follow you wherever you go.

ABOUT THE AUTHOR

Sandra Anne Taylor is an international speaker, counselor, and corporate consultant who lectures throughout the world on the power of consciousness and personal energy. This is Sandra's fifth book with Hay House. *Secrets of Success,* co-authored with Sharon Klingler, explored the holistic nature of attraction and manifestation. *28 Days to a More Magnetic Life* is a handy, pocket-sized book that offers daily techniques and affirmations to help anyone shift their energy on a regular basis. Sandra's *New York Times* best-selling book *Quantum Success* is receiving worldwide acclaim for its enlightening and comprehensive approach to the field of attraction and achievement. Rich in practical application and easy to-understand principles, *Quantum Success* has been called "the real science of consciousness creation."

Sandra's first book, *Secrets of Attraction,* applied the Universal laws to the pursuit of love. Her in-depth nine-CD audio seminar, *Act to Attract,* is the first audio program relating the principles of modern science to the experience of romantic attraction.

For more than 25 years, Sandra was a counselor in a private psychology practice, working with individuals and couples in the treatment of anxiety, depression, addiction, and relationship issues. She teaches the principles of quantum psychology—the powerful connection between mind and manifestation—bringing exceptional clarity and practicality to the science of personal attraction. She has been interviewed on television and radio all over the world and in many national magazines, including *Cosmopolitan, Woman's World, Family Circle, Today's Black Woman, Redbook,* and *Success* magazine, as well as *New Idea* in Australia. Her books are available in 22 languages and dozens of countries around the globe.

Sandra co-founded (along with Sharon Klingler) Starbringer Associates, a speaker and consultant agency that produces audio seminars for personal, spiritual, and business enhancement. For more information—or to schedule lectures, seminars, or private consultations with Sandra—call: (440) 871-5448, or contact her at:

Sandra Anne Taylor
P.O. Box 362
Avon, OH 44011
www.sandrataylor.net

– or –

Starbringer Associates
871 Canterbury Rd., Unit B
Westlake, OH 44145
www.starbringerassociates.com

⚛ ♂ ♀ $ ⚖

Hay House Titles of Related Interest

YOU CAN HEAL YOUR LIFE, the movie,
starring Louise L. Hay & Friends
(available as a 1-DVD program and an expanded 2-DVD set)
Watch the trailer at: **www.LouiseHayMovie.com**

THE SHIFT, the movie,
starring Dr. Wayne W. Dyer
(available as a 1-DVD program and an expanded 2-DVD set)
Watch the trailer at: **www.DyerMovie.com**

The Answer Is Simple . . . *Love Yourself, Live Your Spirit!*
by Sonia Choquette

The Art of Extreme Self-Care: *Transform Your Life One Month at a Time,* by Cheryl Richardson

Everything You Need to Know to Feel Go(o)d,
by Candace B. Pert, Ph.D., with Nancy Marriott

The Power of Infinite Love & Gratitude: *An Evolutionary Journey to Awakening Your Spirit,* by Dr. Darren R. Weissman

The Power of Intention: *Learning to Co-create Your World Your Way,* by Dr. Wayne W. Dyer

The Spontaneous Healing of Belief:
Shattering the Paradigm of False Limits, by Gregg Braden

The Won Thing: *The "One" Secret to a Totally Fulfilling Life,*
by Peggy McColl

All of the above are available at your local bookstore, or may be ordered by contacting Hay House (see next page).

We hope you enjoyed this Hay House book. If you'd like to receive our online catalog featuring additional information on Hay House books and products, or if you'd like to find out more about the Hay Foundation, please contact:

Hay House, Inc., P.O. Box 5100, Carlsbad, CA 92018-5100

(760) 431-7695 or **(800) 654-5126**
(760) 431-6948 (fax) or **(800) 650-5115 (fax)**
www.hayhouse.com® • www.hayfoundation.org

Published and distributed in Australia by: Hay House Australia Pty. Ltd., 18/36 Ralph St., Alexandria NSW 2015 • *Phone:* 612-9669-4299 *Fax:* 612-9669-4144 • www.hayhouse.com.au

Published and distributed in the United Kingdom by: Hay House UK, Ltd., 292B Kensal Rd., London W10 5BE • *Phone:* 44-20-8962-1230 • *Fax:* 44-20-8962-1239 • www.hayhouse.co.uk

Published and distributed in the Republic of South Africa by: Hay House SA (Pty), Ltd., P.O. Box 990, Witkoppen 2068 • *Phone/Fax:* 27-11-467-8904 • info@hayhouse.co.za • www.hayhouse.co.za

Published in India by: Hay House Publishers India, Muskaan Complex, Plot No. 3, B-2, Vasant Kunj, New Delhi 110 070 • *Phone:* 91-11-4176-1620 • *Fax:* 91-11-4176-1630 • www.hayhouse.co.in

Distributed in Canada by: Raincoast, 9050 Shaughnessy St., Vancouver, B.C. V6P 6E5 • *Phone:* (604) 323-7100 *Fax:* (604) 323-2600 • www.raincoast.com